A POCKET GU

STAKEHOLDERS'

~~MANAGEMENT~~

ENGAGEMENT

George Jucan

Copyright © 2017 Organizational Performance Enablers Network

ALL RIGHTS RESERVED. No parts of this work covered by the copyright herein may be reproduced, transmitted, stored or used in any form or by any means graphic, electronic or mechanical, including but not limited to photocopying, recording, scanning, digitizing, taping, web distribution, information networks, or information storage and retrieval systems, except as permitted under Section 107 or 108 of the 1976 United States Copyright Act (as amended), without the prior permission of the author.

ISBN-13: 9781973146247

ISBN-10: 197314624X

DEDICATION

To my daughters, Andra and Cristiana, for being my source of strength and inspiration.

To my wife, Claudia, for your understanding of long hours spent studying and researching.

To my parents, Toader and Alexandrina, for teaching me that hard work always pays off.

And to all the people I ever worked with – I learned something from each and every one of you.

CONTENTS

Foreword 1

Before We Begin 5

Setting The Stage 7

    The Journey 7

    A New Definition Of Success 8

    Why Bother? 10

    Acknowledgements 12

Understanding People 13

    Johari Window 13

    Maslow's Hierarchy of Needs 14

    Myers Briggs Type Indicator (MBTI) 14

    Triarchic Theory of Intelligence 15

    David Kolb's Learning Styles 16

    Summary 17

Know Your Stakeholders 18

    Identify Who's Whom 20

    Analyze And Evaluate 22

    Useful Taxonomies 25

    Summary 28

Plan Stakeholder Engagement 30

    SEAM 31

    Define Activities 33

    A Wholistic Approach 38

  The Plan 40

  Summary 42

Engage Stakeholders 44

  A New Communication Paradigm 45

  Prevent And Extinguish Fires 49

  Effective Involvement 52

  Your Most Valuable Tools 54

  Summary 56

Monitor Engagement 58

  Document Everything 59

  Engagement Dashboards 60

  Adjust Your Strategies 67

  Summary 68

Top 5 Tips For Effective Engagement 70

  Change ~~Management~~ Enablement 70

  First Agree On Processes 71

  Single Version Of The Truth 73

  Enable Voluntary Compliance 74

  Avoid Roadblocks 76

Conclusions 78

About The Author 81

Bibliography 83

"COMING TOGETHER IS A BEGINNING.
KEEPING TOGETHER IS PROGRESS.
WORKING TOGETHER IS SUCCESS. "

HENRY FORD

FOREWORD

While the triple constraint has long since become an obsolete concept, the reality is that scope and quality are pitted against time and cost. But is that all there is to project management? Not at all, there are many other influences on the success of project management, the largest of which is people and their impact. For large projects, there has been the management endeavor of "Public Relations" that, when you come to think of it, is really a communications exercise. But in any case, that exercise is only "one-way".

Today, all of the people associated with a project can be considered as Stakeholders to varying degrees. That is, they may range from those responsible for the project's conception and implementation, to those who will be, or conceive themselves to be, impacted by the outcome of the project, to those who are only marginally affected. And, of course, the larger the project, the larger is the number of stakeholders. Alas, not all stakeholders will view the project in the same positive light but, nevertheless, their collective impression will determine the perceived level of project success.

Now it is evident that more and more professionals are speaking up in the recent years about moving away from the simplistic view of project management. Instead, they are focusing more on customers' and stakeholders' satisfaction as a better measure of project success. Indeed, starting with ISO 21500 and PMI's PMBOK Guide – 5th Edition, Project Stakeholder Management has been introduced as an essential and integral part of project management. That is, as a part of best practices to be applied in most projects most of the time. Consequently, this area of interest has continued to grow and expand.

However, is it realistic to think that Stakeholders can be "Managed" in the first place? With the possible exception of the project manager's own team, Author George Jucan thinks not. In fact, George makes this startlingly clear on the very cover of his book by calling it "*A Pocket Guide to Stakeholder's ~~Management~~ Engagement*". Note the crossing out of the word "Management".

Of course, George is quite right. No doubt from his own experience on large projects, especially in the political arena, you cannot "manage" people in the hierarchy above you – like those responsible for proper project framework, governance, or even the project's direct sponsor. But what you can, and must, do is engage them to provide positive support. Hence a much better label for the exercise is "Stakeholder Engagement" and, as such, is getting increased attention.

George Jucan's *Pocket Guide* adds a unique perspective to this growing body of knowledge by adding to the theoretical discussion specific practical advice derived from his 25 years of managing successful projects. For example, trying to persuade most stakeholders to adhere to formal processes is both extremely difficult and time consuming. Instead, adopt practices that make sense so that some discipline is self-imposed. Likewise, while the program or project manager must set the rules of the game, it is far better to start with the bare minimum, and add more if really needed. Further, always be on the lookout for external signs of change, because in the project "Changes are good, unmanaged changes are bad!"

Generally following the PMBOK® Guide's structure of the stakeholders knowledge area, this work guides the reader through stakeholders' identification and analysis, planning for their engagement and executing the plan, as well as monitoring the engagement and adjusting for increased efficiency. But this is not just a training material on PMBOK Guide – it is a truly practical guide based on his real-life personal experiences.

Each Chapter is focused on the critical elements that should be done for effective stakeholders' engagement. George's practical advice is supported by examples from the author's personal experience, and the specific tools and "tricks of the trade" that he actually uses in his day-to-day practice. Readers should find his actual examples of engagement objectives, his samples of activities defined for each such objective, as well as for each stakeholder or class of stakeholders, most valuable.

For example, George describes a Stakeholders' Map that combines the relative static stakeholders' profile and attributes with the dynamic aspect of their relationships. This has a distinct advantage over traditional stakeholder analysis and classification models that focus on the attributes of each individual stakeholder – but miss the context of the other stakeholders in the environment.

You may find that many authors minimize monitoring and control processes by characterizing them as simply "keeping an eye on changes and modifying your plans accordingly". In contrast, George goes well beyond that, not only with practical advice on how to do just that, but also by presenting the engagement dashboards that he uses for both simple and complex projects. These include: Still To Go Index (STGI); The Heat Map; Stakeholders Activities Performance Index (SAPI) and Stakeholders Engagement Performance Index (SEPI).

Finally, George's 6-point mantra is worth emphasizing thus:
1. Project success is measured in stakeholder satisfaction;
2. Stakeholders need to be "part of the team" to truly support the project;
3. Stakeholders' happiness is directly proportional to their ability to exercise change;
4. Change is the only constant throughout the entire project – build processes based on enabling change, not against it;
5. Enabling change allows to deliver what they really need, not what they thought they wanted when the project started; and
6. Meeting the stakeholders needs results in a successful project.

In conclusion, unlike so many professional books, George has made his *A Pocket Guide to Stakeholders'* ~~Management~~ *Engagement* very easy to read, almost like a memory jogger. Keep it handy for your next project.

R. Max Wideman

FCSCE, FEIC, FICE, FPMI, FCMI

Max Wideman is a defining personality that shaped the project management discipline in what we know today. From leading the publication in 1987 of the very first "The PMBoK" (The Project Management Body of Knowledge) to the numerous books, international standards, articles and speeches, and his world-famous PM Glossary (the most extensive collection of PM terms freely available), Max's work has influenced generations of project professionals around the globe.

More information about Max Wideman's contribution to project management discipline on http://www.maxwideman.com.

BEFORE WE BEGIN

The first question I would ask if I were in your shoes would be "Why should I spend my time reading what this guy has to say?" The answer is quite simple – because it's always better to learn from someone else's mistakes rather than from your own.

And while I'm now considered quite successful at dealing with complex stakeholder environments, it was not always the case – I did my fair share of mistakes in dealing with people involved in my projects, and learned from them. And hopefully, by reading what I discovered in the process you will be able to obtain the gain without feeling the pain.

As many of you, I am what it's called an "accidental project manager". I started as a technical specialist, but rather soon I moved into team lead positions. To be effective I started to read about management and leadership, and I came across project management as a discipline – and I was hooked.

My personality profiles showed that I'm a highly action-oriented person that carefully analyses a situation and plans a course of action without going in an excruciating amount of details. The emotional intelligence component was less developed though, the consideration for what others may or may not feel at the time.

In my early years as a project manager this created quite a few problems, as I could not understand why others are not performing as I am – especially that I never asked anyone else to do something that I wasn't doing already. Not being a natural skill for me, it took a lot of time and effort to develop my emotional quotient and be able to understand and connect with the emotional side of the people.

Through work and conferences and social networking I realized how many others are struggling with the same issues as I did, and tried to help. As a member of the Core Team for the Fifth Edition of PMI's PMBOK® Guide I was one of the advocates of separating the Stakeholders Management as a distinct Knowledge Area from Communications. Now, project managers reading it have at least an idea that they should pay attention to stakeholders, as they do for scope, budget, schedule, risk, quality etc.

For years I've been presenting at conferences my approach to obtaining appropriate stakeholders engagement in projects. That session evolved into a workshop, and finally in this book that I'm now sharing with you.

The material includes a generic foundation, to make sure that key concepts are not missed, as well as my personal approach and useful tips and tricks. Moreover, while primarily addressed to Project Managers, almost everything in this book is also applicable to any stakeholders for any type of endeavor – after all, they are people with interests that may or may not support your objectives and may or may not prevent you from obtaining them.

I also included examples to highlight issues and demonstrate concepts – as always, any similarities with real people or organizations are absolutely unintentional. While highly unlikely for anyone to truly know the real-life scenario that inspired my example, the facts and situations presented are so common that most likely occurred even in your personal experience.

Finally, please let me know your thoughts about this book. You are my stakeholders, and your feedback is really appreciated. Please connect with me by email at GJucan@OPEnablers.Net, or find the book online and post your comments there – best learning happens from each other, and everyone has something important to say!

SETTING THE STAGE

Any good conversation starts with a preamble to create an environment in which people are comfortable to tackle difficult subjects, and this should not be an exception. So before we start talking about how to engage project stakeholders to benefit the project – in fact, before even defining the concept of "stakeholder" – let's spend a bit of time setting the stage for a meaningful conversation.

THE JOURNEY

Before we begin, I'd like to take you back a couple of years – when you were about 5 years of age and people were asking you "What do you want to be when you grow up?" Of course you wanted to be a doctor, teacher, firefighter, airplane pilot and so on, and hopefully you've been able to pursue that dream.

Most likely you went to school and got a job, and started the daily grind to pay the mortgage, bills, kids' expenses etc. And because you're reading this book, I would wager to say that at one point your boss realized that you're better at making other people work rather than doing the work yourself, and suddenly you got assigned as the project manager.

Well, now if you're a project manager you wanted to know what is it all about – so you picked up a book, or searched online and the first thing you came about was the "triple constraint" (sometimes called the "iron triangle" as well).

The classic definition of project success is to deliver the full scope (at adequate quality), in time and within budget.

Knowing what to do to achieve success, you started delivering projects. And to get better you started to read more about it, take training courses, attend conferences and so on to become a better project manager – same as thousands and thousands of others in the same situation like you.

However, research shows a disturbing fact. For example, information published by Standish Group in CHAOS Manifesto over the years regarding how many projects can be considered successful shows that there is no significant improvement in achieving success.

Over the last almost 20 years roughly 30% of projects are successful, while 50% of them are challenged in some way and about 20% fail outright. And every year the variations are within couple of percentage points, but fairly constant as a trend over the years.

If only 1 in 3 projects can really be considered a success it would be expected for the executive ranks to pay much more attention, in a world where wasting corporate money like this could bring about the demise of the organization, or at least the top-level executives.

However, while talking with stakeholders and organizational decision factors we certainly don't get this gloomy image – they feel that much more projects are actually successful. In such case, one stands to wonder: are we really using the correct definition for success?

A NEW DEFINITION OF SUCCESS

The reality is that any project longer than a few weeks will encounter some sort of change from the approved scope, time and cost. Change is the only constant of the corporate environment today – it is the norm, not the exception for projects to need to adjust to changes and re-baseline several times the triple constraint.

There is no way to predict in details what will happen throughout the duration of the project. If we would be able to predict the future we would not have to work anymore – we would just play the lottery for a living! So every plan, every estimate that we prepare is nothing more than an educated guess of how the future will unfold – but a guess nevertheless.

The assumptions we make in our planning and estimating will be later confirmed or invalidated. As the project evolves, scope, time and cost are always changing throughout the project to respond to environmental variations, or to reflect a better understanding of the needs to be addressed.

At the end of day, any project is undertaken to address some needs of the organization. In most cases, these needs cannot be fully and completely described when the project begins – they are like onions, once you peel off a layer you discover another one underneath, and another one, and another one…

And even if you could perfectly describe the needs at the beginning, it's very likely that they will evolve or transform throughout the project duration – the world keeps spinning, and the organization and its environment keep changing, and the project objectives will change with them.

This creates a problem when the project is seen through the "triple constraint" perspective, as the underlying fundamentals of the estimate keep changing. Even having available tools like "integrated change management" and "re-baselining", most project managers will try to maintain the "triple constraint" unchanged for the entire project duration.

But let's go back to the projects you ran, or seen in the organizations you worked for. Can you recall projects that maybe were delivered a bit late, cost more and did not quite delivered all the T's and I's from the requirements document, but everyone remembers them as a great success? How about projects completed in time, in budget and delivering approved scope that were shelved and never really used? Were these considered a success?

Reality is that pleased stakeholders will ignore small delays, cost overruns and even accept workarounds and minor inconveniences. As long as they are pleased with what they got for that they invested in the project, and they had a pleasant experience being part of it, they will consider it a successful project.

There is a growing trend in project management of going beyond the triple constraint. For example, Max Wideman in Chapter 17 of *A Field Guide to Project Management* (Cleland, 2004) states that *the real measure of project success is the level of "customer satisfaction" in the final product.*

However, customers are not the only ones that should be happy with the project deliverables – other stakeholders are important as well (if the CFO is not happy, tough luck getting the budget approved for your next

9

project!). So instead of the "triple constraint" maybe we should consider that:

A project is only as successful as the stakeholders think it is!

A project is considered as being successful if, after the dust has settled, is remembered that it delivered <u>perceived</u> value to the stakeholders. It's not ever really about <u>real</u> value (in absolute, objective terms), but about how the delivered value impacts and relates with the stakeholders expectations from the project. Delivered value and associated project success is extremely subjective – it's all in the eyes of the beholder!

WHY BOTHER?

So, if success is not an objective set of numbers assembled in the "triple constraint", but a subjective perception of each stakeholder about how his/her particular needs were fulfilled by the value produced by the project, it probably is very complicated to measure project success, right? Well, it certainly is complicated!

Influencing people's perspective about the project deliverables requires a lot of work, not only at acceptance time but throughout the entire project duration. It requires not only a lot of communication, but also paying a lot of attention to all the verbal and non-verbal signals that they send – which sometimes can be really exhausting!

But you have to remember, despite all the machines, tools, techniques, methodologies, at the end of day:

Projects are done by people, with people, and for people

- team
- partners
- clients

People will make or break a project, and people are complex beings that perceive facts or situations through their individual frameset of values. Past experiences, accumulated knowledge and preconceptions alter people's perception of reality and makes them sometimes very difficult to understand – unless there's a significant overlap between the corresponding values framesets.

This is not a psychology paper so I'll not go into any details, but there is a significant body of work out there clearly demonstrating that people hear what they want to hear, and see what they want to see! A classic example is the rotating dancer that people will see moving either clockwise or counter-clockwise, and they will be convinced that they are correct (and anyone saying differently is wrong).

However, people's confidence in their own perception can be exploited by a savvy project manager. By highlighting certain details you can focus their attention where you want them to look, and influence their "own" opinion – it's more efficient to make them see by themselves what you want them to see, rather than trying to convince them to accept your version of reality!

Using the rotating dancer as an example, it's almost impossible to convince someone seeing the dancer rotating one way that in fact it moves the other way. In the figure below, if you only focus on the middle picture you could picture it either with the left foot up or with the right foot up, so it could rotate either way. But adding some details you can influence people to see the dancer either with the left foot up (left image) or with the right foot up (right image) – and once they see the details you're focusing their attention to it will be almost impossible to see it any other way!

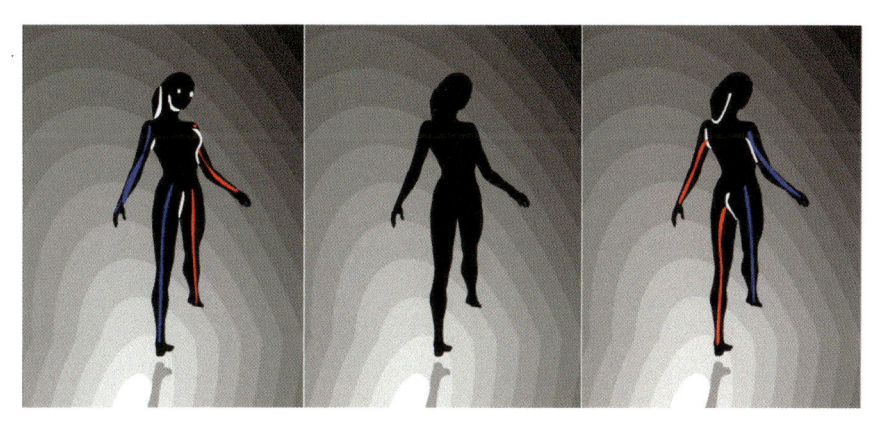

It is not easy, and it usually requires a significant time and effort investment to make people see things your way, especially if you want them to think that is their own perception – and therefore accepting it by default! However, if you can help them see the value that the project delivered for them, it will go a long way toward perceiving the project as a success!

ACKNOWLEDGEMENTS

There is significant literature out there dealing with stakeholders relationships, including Gower Handbook of People in Project Management (Scott, 2013) and Managing Project Stakeholders: Building a Foundation to Achieve Project Goals (Roeder, 2013).

A special mention regarding the standardization efforts in project, programme and portfolio management, specifically ISO 21500:2012 - Guidance on project management (ISO\TC258, 2012) and PMI's A Guide to the Project Management Body of Knowledge (PMBOK® Guide)— Sixth Edition (PMI - PMBOK Guide, 2017). Both include best practices collected from practitioners around the world, including for the stakeholder management domain.

The sections of this book are closely aligned with the aforementioned standards to avoid creating any more confusion in the practitioners' world. However, this book goes well beyond the summary statements included in the standards, and enriches the topics with practical considerations and personal experience.

UNDERSTANDING PEOPLE

The previous chapter ended with a – hopefully convincing – argument to invest time and effort in understanding the people important for the project, particularly how they perceive the reality, how they think, act and communicate. There is plenty of documentation available out there, so this chapter will only do a high-level introduction to some of the useful tools available (most even free).

JOHARI WINDOW

A simple and useful model for illustrating and improving self-awareness, and mutual understanding between individuals within a group was introduced in 1955 by psychologists Joseph Luft and Harrington Ingham (Luft & Ingham, 1955).

It is based on a self-assessment and external feedback using a predefined list of adjectives. Depending on the selection by the person or by assessors, the attributes are placed on a grid to define four regions:

- *known by oneself and known by others* - open area, open self, free area, free self, or 'the arena'
- *unknown by oneself but known by others* - blind area, blind self, or 'blindspot'
- *known by oneself that others do not know* - hidden area, hidden self, avoided area, avoided self or 'facade'
- *unknown by oneself and also unknown by others* - unknown area, unknown self

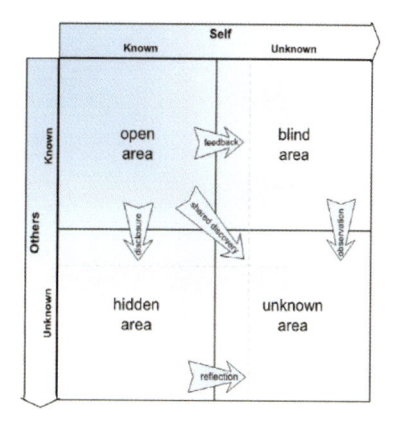

The primary purpose of this method is to expand one's open area, but understanding how a person perceives itself and the gaps with other people's perception can be useful in understanding the frameset of values used by that person during communication.

MASLOW'S HIERARCHY OF NEEDS

Introduced initially as a journal article (Maslow, A Theory of Human Motivation, 1943) and fully defined in 1954 by Abraham Maslow (Maslow, Motivation and Personality, 1954), this extremely well-known model organizes human needs as a pyramid in a hierarchy of importance, starting with the most basic needs to sustain life.

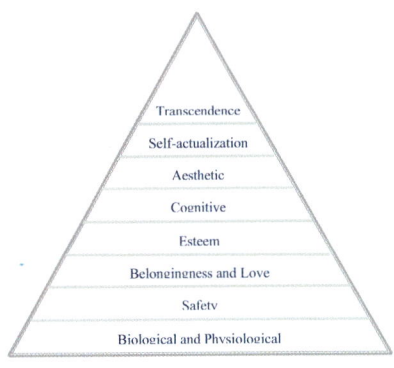

Maslow's theory predicates that more abstract needs emerge only when higher-priority (basic) needs have been satisfied. Moreover, satisfied needs no longer influence behavior, and as such money and other tangible incentives are not the only avenues to motivate people - the need to participate, to be recognized, to be creative, and to experience a sense of worth are better motivators for mid-career, experienced people.

While subsequent research studies indicate that at any point in time an individual is driven by a mix of motivators, Maslow's model is still the most used to assess what is *most likely* to motivate a person based on the stage in life / career – a.k.a. what needs have been already fulfilled or are the current focus for that individual.

MYERS BRIGGS TYPE INDICATOR (MBTI)

Expanding the theory of psychological types introduced in the 1920s by Carl G. Jung (Jung, 1921), Katharine Cook Briggs and her daughter Isabel Briggs Myers introduced the Myers–Briggs Type Indicator (MBTI) as a self-assessment designed to highlight the psychological foundations of how people perceive their environment, and the

(E) Extraversion	or	Introversion (I)
(S) Sensing	or	INtuition (N)
(T) Thinking	or	Feeling (F)
(J) Judging	or	Perceiving (P)

motivators of their decision-making process. (Cook Briggs & Briggs Myers, 1962)

MBTI is *not* a measurement of intelligence or competence, but a tool to understand an individual's personality and predict the most likely behavior in reaction to the environment stimuli. While critics indicate that the MBTI is not extremely reliable as the self-assessment may lead to different results based on person's momentary state of mind, the MBTI is a very popular tool in the business sector.

TRIARCHIC THEORY OF INTELLIGENCE

Robert Sternberg's definition of human intelligence is based on an individual's ability to adapt to changes in the environment (Sternberg, 1985). Sternberg defines three types of intelligence, specifically:

- *Componential / Analytical* – the ability to resolve problems and make decisions based on:
  - Metacomponents: govern how the mind works
  - Performance components: actually carry out actions
  - Knowledge-acquisition components: obtain new information

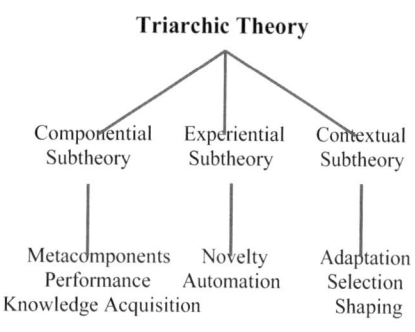

Triarchic Theory

Componential Subtheory — Metacomponents, Performance, Knowledge Acquisition

Experiential Subtheory — Novelty, Automation

Contextual Subtheory — Adaptation, Selection, Shaping

- *Experiential / Creative* – the ability to perform tasks is located on a continuum between:
  - Novelty: find new ways of solving a task
  - Automation: the task can now be done with little thought
- *Practical / Contextual* – the ability to react to the external environment involves:
  - Adaptation: change oneself to better adjust to surroundings
  - Shaping: changing the environment to better suit the needs
  - Selection: finding a completely new alternate environment

Understanding the specific strengths of various people involved in the project allows to tailor their assignments (project team), and also adapt the interactions to their specific type of intelligence.

For example, to obtain approvals you would want to make it as effortless as possible for each of them – so for some a high-level presentation may be enough, while others would be better reached by inviting them to attend a hands-on demo.

DAVID KOLB'S LEARNING STYLES

David Kolb body of work is based on his concept that "Learning is the process whereby knowledge is created through the transformation of experience" (Kolb, 1984). His learning theory defines four distinct learning styles (or preferences), defined across the following dimensions:

- *Perception dimension*:
    - Concrete experience: Looking at things as they are, without any change, in raw detail.
    - Abstract conceptualization: Looking at things as concepts and ideas, after a degree of processing that turns the raw detail into an internal model.
- *Processing dimension*:
    - Active experimentation: Taking what they have concluded and trying it out to prove that it works.
    - Reflective observation: Taking what they have concluded and watching to see if it works.

Of particular importance is Kolb's "cycle of learning" in which basic experiences are analyzed and transformed into abstract concepts that can be applied to other tasks – and as such creating new experiences that restart the cycle.

SUMMARY

This chapter presented a few of the tools that I like and use to understand the people I interact with, because each of them provides different perspectives. People are at different career levels, have different personalities, come from different backgrounds etc., so they are both very different and very complex – like diamonds, and each tool will shine the light on only one facet so you'll need a diverse toolset to be able to understand their full intricacies.

And you do need to understand them because – as discussed in previous chapter – the project success depends on their perception about your project. And you'll need individual and group methods able to target the specifics of each stakeholder in order to ensure that the perception they have is the one you want them to have.

You absolutely have to produce the project deliverables, of course. But producing without presenting them, in the hope the stakeholders will take the time to appreciate them, does not guarantee a successful project. You must actively showcase the project's accomplishments, and use multiple methods such as presentations, demos, workshops, brainstorming, reports etc. in order to reach every stakeholder their own way.

To do so efficiently you'll also need as many interpersonal skills as you can master: empathy, communication, negotiation, influencing, persuasion etc. But let's not get ahead of ourselves, we'll talk about all of these in the next chapters of this book as we discuss the main activities the project managers must perform related to stakeholders.

KNOW YOUR STAKEHOLDERS

I used the term "project stakeholders" several times up to now, without ever defining the term. If you're reading this book I would assume that you have at least a decent understanding of the concept – otherwise why would you be interesting in dealing with them?

However, let's make sure we are all on the same wavelength, as there are some minor variations between some of the definitions used by various standards and methodologies.

> **Project stakeholders are individuals, groups or organizations who may affect, be affected by, or perceive themselves to be affected by a decision, activity, or outcome of a project**

While all the time there will be people interacting with the project, it is important to differentiate when they act on their own name, or when they represent the interests of a group (e.g. Finance, Quality Assurance) or even an entire organization (e.g. a supplier in a contractual relationship). People behave and act differently when it's their own skin in the game or when they are shielded in a protective cocoon.

This is not a psychology book to fully explain why this difference in behavior, but only to prove the point let's look at risk propensity – popular belief is that a person will be more risk adverse in a business context, but studies clearly show that an individual risking his/her own money, reputation etc. will always be more cautious than when the potential pitfalls are to be absorbed by an entire organization. Moreover, studies also show that people will always protect more their own interests rather than organizational interests that they may or may not agree with.

As such, while the relationship will always be with an actual person, from a project perspective it's important to know if the stakeholder is the individual or the group/organization he/she represents.

Until couple of years ago, the definition only included "may affect or be affected by" – it is quite obvious that you need to take care of the people that can impact (either obstruct or help) the project, or that will have to accept the change brought about by the project.

The interesting part is "perceive themselves to be affected by" – if there is no real impact to these people, why should you waste your time dealing with them at all? Well, couple of years ago a windmill farm project in Ontario, Canada was scrapped because people in the area considered that destroying the beauty of the horizon line will bring down their properties value.

They were located miles away from the site, and nobody considered them as a potential stakeholder – but they perceived themselves as being impacted, organized a public action committee and eventually cancelled the project – after quite a lot of funds were already sunk in it.

Especially in large, public-facing projects it's not always easy to anticipate who may consider themselves as being impacted by the project – but spending some time thinking about it may save a lot of trouble later!

Lastly, the definition used to refer only at the whole project through its deliverables, which made project managers to involuntarily focus only on the stakeholders that were engaged for the entire project duration. However, a stakeholder could only be part of a single action or decision – or such action or decision could make the difference between a temporary or a full-project stakeholder, or even not a stakeholder at all.

> *Due to environmental groups' opposition a mining prospecting project in Brazil decided to airlift materials and personnel to the site instead of cutting a dirt road through the forest. The road component had as stakeholder a local community, and cancelling the road took them off the stakeholders list – with the associated economic loss in construction jobs, lodging and accommodations for external personnel etc.*
>
> *The assessment representing the overall project deliverable was not impacted, but a single project decision had a tremendous impact of that specific stakeholder.*

IDENTIFY WHO'S WHOM

It is common sense that the first step is to find who the project stakeholders are. The most efficient way is to withhold any judgment at this time, and simply scan the project environment and list the people, groups or organizations that could impact or be impacted by a decision, activity or outcome of the project.

It is a natural tendency to start to assess a stakeholder as soon as it was identified – we like to know as much as we can about any element of any importance, and the human brain is unconsciously trying to focus and drill-down. However, this switches gears for the brain from "identify" to "analyze", and switching back is not always seamless.

Studies on the brainstorming method clearly indicate that if participants maintain the discovery perspective it produces significantly more comprehensive lists. At this stage the main objective is to no miss anyone of potential significance, so it's best to refrain from any discussions about the identified stakeholders – just list them, there will be a chance to discuss them later on.

In practice there are 2 main approaches used to identify stakeholders: top-down and inside-out.

Top-down approach predicates to start with the Project Sponsor – the most important stakeholder – and ask "whom else should be involved in this project?" to obtain a new set of stakeholders. Then ask each of the stakeholders currently on the list the same question, add any identified individuals to the list, and repeat until no new name is identified.

The inside-out approach uses the "distance" from the project (and correspondingly from the project manager) to focus on each area at a time:

- *Team*: anyone that has to create something or perform any action under the supervision and control of the project manager is a stakeholder – they can clearly impact the project, and sometimes be impacted by its activities, decisions or outcomes.

- *Internal*: any person or group (department, division, team etc.) from within the organization or organizations undertaking the project that provides or enables anything related to the project, or have to do anything because of the outcome of the project (e.g. call center may have an increased calls volume).
- *External*: any third-parties legally independent from your own that could have any touch point with the project – not only suppliers but also the public or local communities, or agencies that issue permits or provide oversight.

The list of identified stakeholders is the beginning of the Stakeholders Register. This is a very unique document, usually represented as a matrix – but while most documents expand vertically (start with a table of content and add detail and new sections), the Stakeholders Register expands horizontally: it starts with a full list of stakeholders but only few "identification" columns, and will continue to add columns (hence expanding horizontally) as you go through the analysis and classification activities.

> *In my first years as a PM I was managing the replacement of a legacy system with a browser-based custom developed solution. During initiation I was introduced to several people from the client's IT department and was told they will be my stakeholders – and if they need anything they may consult others within the client's organization. I failed to hear the alarm, and took those statements at face value.*
>
> *At the first major milestone, we present a demo of the new interface to the client representatives – received enthusiastically by said stakeholders. However, not even 2 days later I get a message about how bad the interface is, how dysfunctional and disorganized is ... Of course, I immediately went on-site to see how things could change completely since the demo.*
>
> *Long story short, they showed the interface demo to some line staff, current users of the legacy system, and they simply tore the new interface apart. But digging a bit deeper, they were really against*

> *the change itself to a new system, and anything anyone would have put in front of them would have triggered the same reaction.*
>
> *Realizing my mistake of ignoring them, I brought in the most vocal critics into a "power users group" (to not take away from the "stakeholder" denomination of the IT folks), to be involved in redesigning and test-driving the new interface.*
>
> *Within weeks, the same people were now the advocates of changing to the new system – because now they were a part of it and they felt it were their change, something they had control over and not something imposed on them by outsiders.*

ANALYZE AND EVALUATE

During the discovery process it was important to focus on simply listing the stakeholders, without any judgment. Now that we have the list, it's time to analyze and document relevant information such as their interests, involvement, interdependencies, influence, and potential impact on project success.

This can be a time consuming activity, especially if there are many identified stakeholders, so why should you do it? Well, unlike other resources that you could potentially get more of (e.g. money, people) time is fixed to 24 hours in a day. As the available hours in a day are limited, you need to make best use of the time to focus on those stakeholders that could bring most benefit or could impact the project the most.

Paraphrasing George Orwell's *Animal Farm* (1945), "all stakeholders are equal, but some are more equal than others" – and these are the ones you should focus more on. But to understand who's who you need to understand their expectations and intrinsic power, and even assess how are they likely to react or respond in various situations, in order to plan how to influence them to enhance their support and mitigate potential negative impacts.

Some aspects of the analysis are reasonable simple – for example, to understand stakeholder expectations you could interview them, or ask them to respond to questionnaires and surveys. While this is a "safe" area and people would normally be willing to discuss it, you must be careful that sometimes people say what they think you expect them to say as opposed to what they truly think.

It is up to you to extract the expectations that they would not state or would not even think that it should be stated. A good method is the "5 why's" – introduced by Sakichi Toyoda (the founder of Toyota Industries), it predicates that by asking 5 times "why?" you should arrive at the root cause of an issue (or fundamental reasoning behind a statement).

Things are getting a bit more complicated when assessing areas such as their interest and involvement in the project, where you have to combine information extracted from stakeholders with your own judgment calls about them. For example, an IT support manager may declare that he/she does not care about a project, but when it's time for the deliverable to be transitioned to operations he/she will certainly start to critique the system's stability and request fixes before accepting it. Or an executive may state that he/she will be deeply involved with the project, but will he/she realistically have the time required to be involved?

The good news about the next step is that you'll uncover fundamental information, actionable to create strategies to deal with the corresponding stakeholders. The bad news is that it's getting more complicated, because it relies completely in your personal assessment of stakeholders' actual influence and their corresponding importance in the project.

At this time your expert judgment will guide you, based on all the information you collected this far and past information from other projects that you know of. You can also seek advice from others, but be very careful how you word your questions and they can be very easily misconstrued and get you in a heap of trouble.

However, the outcomes of this exercise will allow you to determine the appropriate focus required for each stakeholder. Let's think at an executive (with significant positional power) that never gets directly involved in projects, but delegates (sometimes informally) his/her involvement to another person. In this case the stakeholder with high influence is the delegate (his/her recommendations are always approved by the executive), and that's the person you should focus on, not the executive.

> *In an organization I worked for (a while back), there was a person with limited power (low management position) that always tried to get himself involved in almost every project, regardless if it touched or not his area. Moreover, he wanted things done his way, and if they were done otherwise would repeatedly complain to everyone on a senior management position until they got fed up of wasting time in arguments and changed things to stop his complaints.*
>
> *Based on past experience, this person would be a stakeholder even if not officially involved in the project – it fits the "perceive themselves as being impacted by" part of the definition. And frankly, such a stakeholder you ignore at your own peril!*

Finally, let's talk about the Stakeholder Registry that you have to expand now to add all this information. As seen before, some if the comments you need to capture would not be very flattering for the corresponding person – sow what do you do now? If you write down the truth as you see it you may completely destroy the relationship, but if you don't the document is worthless as the most relevant information will be missing!

In smaller projects with a limited number of stakeholders most PMs will only fill in the "neutral" columns, and simply keep in mind the other information. This does not work for large projects with hundreds of stakeholders – plus that for large project most methodologies require to maintain a Stakeholder Registry.

It is an ethical dilemma where you have to balance saying what you think with thinking what you say. In such cases you may want to use 2 registers, one saved in project repository (neutral columns) and one "for your eyes only" (everything else) as seen below:

Category	Name	Department / Organization	Title	Role in Project	Expectations	Involvement	Interest	Influence	Importance

4 your "I"s only

USEFUL TAXONOMIES

For small projects it may be feasible to define a specific strategy for each individual stakeholder, but most projects have tens if not hundreds of stakeholders so they need a type of grouping or classification to define shared strategies. You may still have some personalized touches for the most critical stakeholders – such as the sponsor – but having common strategies for all stakeholders in a certain class will dramatically increase your efficiency.

There are multiple taxonomies out there that classify stakeholders based on one, more or a combination of attributes from the Stakeholder Registry, and I've seen many organizations that defined their own classification model to account for specific particularities.

Maybe the widest used classification model is a type of a 2-dimensional grid, using as axis two of the columns in the Registry, considered relevant for the corresponding project. Most commonly seen matrices are:

- *Power/interest* grid, grouping the stakeholders based on their level of authority ("power") and their level or concern ("interest") regarding the project outcomes
- *Power/influence* grid, grouping the stakeholders based on their level of authority ("power") and their active involvement ("influence") in the project
- *Influence/impact* grid, grouping the stakeholders based on their active involvement ("influence") in the project and their ability to effect changes to the project's planning or execution ("impact")

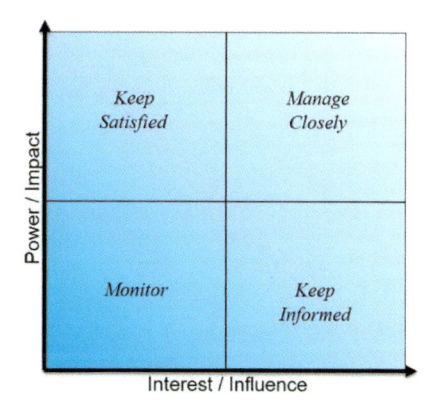

3-dimensional (spatial) models allow for a more refined classification, useful in complex stakeholders environments where a more personalized approach is needed. The most well-known tool in this category is the

Salience model, even if it is a relatively newcomer being first introduced at the end of 20th century (Mitchell, Agle, & Wood, 1997). Defining the classes of stakeholders based on their power (ability to impose their will), urgency (need for immediate attention), and legitimacy (their involvement is appropriate) creates 7 categories to use for classification:

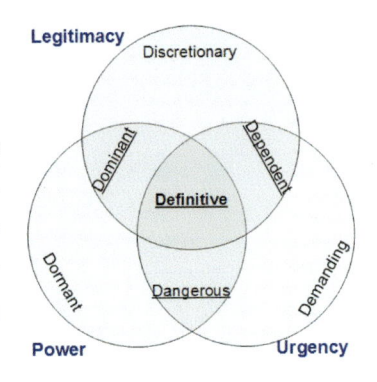

- *Dormant* stakeholders possess power to impose their will on a firm, but by not having a legitimate relationship or an urgent claim, their power remains unused.
- *Discretionary* stakeholders possess the attribute of legitimacy, but they have no power to influence the firm and no urgent claims.
- *Demanding* stakeholders have urgent claims but having neither power nor legitimacy are just noise that could distract the project from its objectives.
- *Dominant* stakeholders have legitimate claims and the ability to act on these claims, but they may or may not ever choose to act on their claims.
- *Dependent* stakeholders have urgent legitimate claims but depend upon other stakeholders for the power necessary to carry out their will.
- *Dangerous* stakeholders have urgent demands and the power to impose them, even if they may be illegitimate with respect to the particular project.
- *Definitive* stakeholders have immediate demands relevant to the project, and the power to impose them into the scope of work.

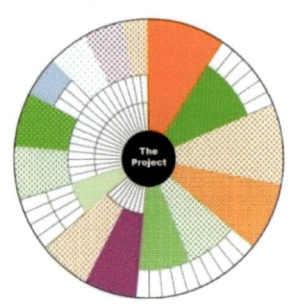

Another 3-dimensional tool based on the power, influence and proximity attributes is the Stakeholder Circle (Weaver & Bourne, 2002). The project is located in the centre of the circle, the radial depth of the segment represents the stakeholder power, the segment width represents the influence, while the proximity is represented through the distance from the centre. A color coding is also used to classify stakeholders in groups.

Personally, I prefer a combined method that I call The Stakeholders' Network. The key differentiator between the Stakeholders' Network and other tools is that it combines the relative static stakeholders' classification with the dynamic aspect of their relationships.

I use a 5-steps scale to classify the state in which a stakeholder is: Unaware, Resistant, Neutral, Supportive or Leading – these are defined in the next Chapter as part of SEAM technique that initially introduced this classification. Moreover, the relationships are classified as well (e.g. trusted advisor, close collaboration, personal friends etc.) to discover influence paths that could be used later on to communicate information or sway decisions toward a favorable outcome for the project.

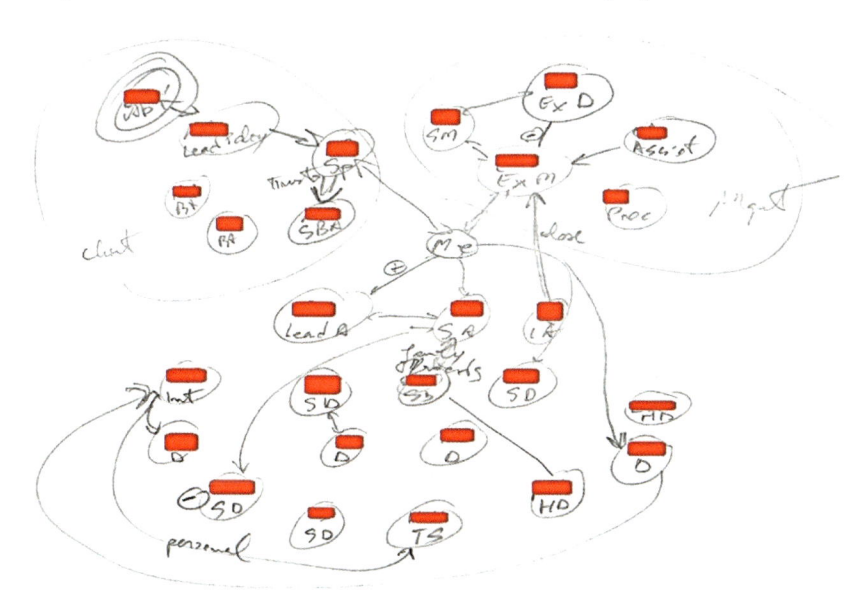

The Stakeholders' Map evolves as new stakeholders are identified and new relationships discovered. From an ethical perspective, as long as this tool is used solely for the benefit of the project and not for personal advantages, this representation does not have to be saved in the common documents repository – it fits the "need to know" criteria, or better said "no need to know"!

27

Regardless of what tool you use, it is important to spend the time to really do a good classification for the identified project stakeholders – it will be of tremendous help for the next step, planning their engagement in the project.

> *I was once called in by a Project Sponsor to help recovering a project going nowhere fast: meeting over meetings with 20-30 people, tens of emails daily with long distribution lists, decisions taking weeks until all comments were addressed...*
>
> *As soon as I reviewed the Stakeholder Register the problem was visible – it was almost as long as the company directory, with no assessment or classification of stakeholders. As such, everyone was involved in everything even if they really did not have any involvement in the corresponding activity or decision. And because they were part of the discussion they felt obligated to contribute to justify their presence, which typically sent the discussion on tangents that ended up having nothing to do with the project.*
>
> *The first step was to organize a half-day workshop with the Sponsor, Project Management and 5 key stakeholders to analyse and classify the project stakeholders. A message was sent to everyone previously involved that measures are taken to reduce the information overflow, and they will only be involved as required, based on a revised schedule and responsibilities matrix.*
>
> *For couple of weeks there was a bit of discontent, but eventually people realized that they are still involved in the items that are really important for them and everyone calmed down. Within 2 months the project was progressing at a normal pace, and everyone's confidence was up again.*

SUMMARY

This chapter presented the succession of steps to identify, analyse and classify the project stakeholders. It is very important to resist the natural impulse to start analysing a stakeholder as soon as identified, keep these as separate and distinct steps in the process.

Focusing strictly on identifying stakeholders will help making sure you don't miss anyone that later on may become critical. If there are many stakeholders on the list after the first step, it may be a good idea to first perform a superficial analysis and apply a simple classification method, such as a 2-dimensional grid. This will normally provide you enough information to define group activities, as described in the next chapter.

However, at least for the ones identified as key stakeholders at the first pass, you may want to apply a more refined analysis method and a more sophisticated classification tool, to be able to define specific activities targeting the people that can make or break your project. These may include individual actions, specifically tailored for these key stakeholders – more details in the next chapter.

PLAN STAKEHOLDER ENGAGEMENT

We are project managers and by definition we love to plan! Working efficiently with stakeholders, especially when you have more than a few, requires systematic action based on a plan, so you need to do the same as for all other knowledge areas: you need to plan. Specifically, you need to define appropriate management strategies to effectively engage project stakeholders to maximize their support and minimize any adverse impacts.

Everything in the project depends on stakeholders, starting with getting the Charter signed to even become a project. As such planning for stakeholders' engagement must happen as early as possible in the project's life-cycle.

It's not accidentally that in PMBOK® Guide 6th Edition (PMI - PMBOK Guide, 2017) the Identify Stakeholders process is defined as part of Initiating Process Group, in parallel with Develop Project Charter. At least a preliminary planning should be done at this time, to effectively engage the key stakeholders – you want them to sign the Charter after all!

It takes a bit of time and effort to assess all the information to create a clear, actionable plan to interact with project stakeholders to maximize their support and minimize resistance. Many – even experienced – project managers still ignore this planning element, relying on their personal charm and past experience to deal with stakeholders when the situation calls for it.

Now, let's think about it for a minute – unless it involves the same person or persons and a very similar situation, how likely is it to be able to apply something from your past experience and get the desired results? On the other hand, planning for potential scenarios provides a range of options to choose from when the time comes.

Not only that you have a better chance to have a suitable course of action already planned for, but also later on – when the issue arises and you're under fire – you will not have to waste time thinking it through to define your options when hours may be critical.

And, in fact, you will have way less fires to put out if you planned carefully some proactive measures and followed it through. It should not need much explanation that if you built a solid relationship when times were good, it would be a solid foundation to leverage when the storm hits.

> *Planning for all the possible scenarios for all stakeholders is clearly an impossible task – this is NOT what planning is about! Very similar with the approach taken for risk management, you have to imagine as much as possible everything that could go wrong, and then apply a likelihood and impact rating to select the ones you actually want to define a strategy for.*
>
> *Between selecting only a part of potential issues to include in planning and using individual but also stakeholder groups as discussed in previous chapter, the task becomes much more feasible – in fact, no more complicated than the risk planning exercise!*

Finally, when planning for stakeholders' engagement please remember that it must happen throughout the entire project life cycle, from day 0 to the very end. Moreover, the level and type of engagement varies based on their needs, interests and potential impact on project success, and all these are changing in time based on the project phase.

SEAM

The Stakeholder Engagement Assessment Matrix (SEAM) is arguably the most popular tool for a visual representation of current and target state for each stakeholder. While I encountered couple of variations, it typically uses the following potential states:

- *Unaware*: unaware of the project and its potential personal or organizational impacts
- *Resistant*: aware of the project and its potential impacts, and resistant to change
- *Neutral*: aware of the project, yet neither supportive nor resistant
- *Supportive*: aware of the project and its potential impacts, and supportive of the change
- *Leading*: aware of the project and its potential impacts, and actively engaged in ensuring the project is successful

Based on the outcomes of Identify Stakeholders process you now know what the current state of each stakeholder is. The next step is to define in what state each stakeholder needs to be in order to be most effective for the project objectives.

This is where your expert judgment comes in, with potential guidance from other trusted advisors – keyword being "trusted", as this may be sensitive information that could be easily misconstrued. However, defining the target state is usually based on a number of assumptions, and testing your assumptions with others what interacted with the corresponding stakeholder is extremely beneficial.

In some cases it's very simple – let's say you have a project sponsor that is neutral to the project (may have been assigned without having a direct interest in the project, or is simply too busy to get involved in your project). It's obvious that neutral is not a desired state for a sponsor, so the target state should be leading or at least supportive.

In other cases it may be a bit more complicated – let's take an unaware stakeholder. This may be the desired state too, but also you may want to prevent that stakeholder from turning into resistant by proactive communication to transition him/her into neutral or even supportive.

A typical Stakeholder Engagement Assessment Matrix is represented in the following figure:

Stakeholder	Unaware	Resistant	Neutral	Supportive	Leading
1			C		D
2				C / D	
3		C		D	
4	C		D		
5		C	D		

C = Current state   D = Desired state

Finally, please remember that the SEAM represents a point-in-time, as the current as well as the desired state for a stakeholder may evolve throughout the project. For example, a neutral stakeholder that now moved into a supportive state may require a change in strategy to further advance to leading. Also, stakeholders that may be needed to lead during project initiation phase may be required only in a supportive state once the execution phase begins.

> *Tip: this is not a document suitable for the shared documents repository, accessible to everyone part of the project - some people may take issue to being called "resistant", even if they know it's true.*

DEFINE ACTIVITIES

The most delicate part of planning for stakeholders' engagement is defining activities to get each relevant stakeholder to the desired state. This requires a delicate balance between group activities, targeting a class of stakeholders as defined during assessment, with individual activities targeting the specifics of each individual.

Before talking about what activities you can do, let's focus first on the main objectives you are trying to achieve while dealing with stakeholders:

- *Communicate information* to eliminate the stress created by unknowns – an uneasy feeling from lack of information, sometimes fueled by rumors, will make them dissociate from the project.
- *Obtain information* about the current state of facts, which represent your project's starting point – sometimes they don't even think that you need to know it, so keep asking questions!
- *Understand their needs and expectations* of how their world will look like when the project is complete – it may not have been perfectly captured in the requirements.
- *Adjust their expectations* to be realistic in terms of what the project is supposed to deliver – everyone wants the moon, but if all they need is to be able to see when it's night outside maybe all they really need is a lamppost...
- *Obtain their support* for allocation of resources (funding, time dedicated to the project etc.) – some in their own control (their own

33

time for example) and some for which they can put pressure on executives (so you don't have to ask for them)

- *Minimize potential negativity* and outright resistance – best results are obtained by turning their attention to the most listened radio station in the world, WII FM (What's In It For Me)!
- *Get them actively involved* in the project to feel invested in and a part of it – nobody will declare it a failure if they were a part of it!
- *Obtain their guidance* to steer the project where it really needs to end up, not where it was stated at the initiation – the world has surely changed in the meantime!
- *Secure approvals* for various deliverables and the project as a whole – the sign-off should be a simple formality, you should build for approval throughout the entire project to have no surprises at the end.

Now it's time to focus on what you can do to achieve these objectives. Of course, it's most efficient to push as much as possible to common activities targeting an entire class of stakeholders, and only fine-tune objectives achievement for each stakeholder with couple personalized activities.

Because group activities target a diverse audience, it is very important to be carefully crafted based on a very clear objective. Once you know what you want to obtain, you should plan how the activity will unfold – of course, things will never happen exactly as envisioned, but at least you'll have a baseline to identify and minimize deviations. Some of the most used group activities are:

- *Workshops* – typically used to collect information about stakeholders' needs and expectations, but sometimes mixed with some decision-making methods to immediately act on the collected information. They can be focused, with participants of a similar nature (e.g. all members of purchasing department, or all project managers from the various companies involved in the same project), or cross-functional, with participants providing multiple perspectives (e.g. business and IT).
- *Brainstorming* – used to generate ideas that eventually will become decisions. Together with its more structured "cousin", the Nominal Group Technique, brainstorming is an excellent avenue to actively engage stakeholders in steering the project in the right direction – and

because they are part of the decisions they have no choice than to approve the outcomes at the end!

- *Meetings* – most useful avenue to both disseminate and also obtain information, obtaining support and addressing any issues that could negatively impact the project. To be effective you need to have the right people around the table (representing all interested parties, prepared to discuss the topics, and with authority to make decisions), keep the discussions focused on the pre-announced topic, secure expressed commitment to conclusions (lack of opposition does not equal approval), and follow up to ensure that the action items actually get done.

- *Surveys, polls, questionnaires* – the only way to obtain information from very numerous and potentially disperse stakeholders, but limited to predefined questions and answers. The addition of comment fields allows collecting some unstructured / unscripted information, but lacks the buildup obtained through interaction with other people's perspectives. The wording of the questions and answers is critical, as it will influence the participants' responses.

- *Presentations* – usually a vehicle to distribute information, mitigate expectations and sometimes to trigger action or decisions. As these tap into more communication capabilities than written documents they are becoming increasingly preferred to ensure that the message actually gets across to the audience. There is significant information on the Internet about efficiently using words, audio, video, body language etc. to deliver effective presentations.

- *Reports, memos, briefings* – the traditional way of distributing information to various audiences, creating a "paper trail" but also ensuring that the information is captured in a repository – not always easy to retrieve though! These days they are also used in electronic format, with emails, forum posts and blogs fulfilling the same basic function as the traditional paper-based information vehicles.

- *Simulations, demonstrations* – increasingly used for active engagement in experiential decision-making by exploring different potential scenarios. They are also extremely effective in managing stakeholders' expectations by showcasing alternate ways of fulfilling their needs, which may be quite different of what they envisioned initially. Used wisely they can also eliminate uncertainties, increase confidence and minimize resistance toward the project's objectives.

Of course, people react differently to group activities based on their own particularities, as discussed in the previous chapter. At least for key stakeholders that could make or break the project, there is a clear need to add a personal touch to bring them into the desired state as discussed in the previous section. Some of the individual activities that could be performed are:

- *Interviews* – gathering information from and understanding the objectives of key stakeholders may warrant spending time on 1-on-1 meetings with them. Being able to carry on an unobstructed conversation, without other interjections that may alter or distract from the conveyed message, would allow you to understand not only publicly stated positions but the deeper reasons, concerns and personal objectives that you need to cater to in order to secure their support.
- *Briefings* – while written briefing notes have usually a larger distribution, in-person briefings usually target a single executive that has a key role in the project. Usually supported by a briefing note or report, a briefing allows you to convey more sensitive information that may not be appropriate to be captured in a written format. Used effectively, briefings also allow you to influence executive decisions toward benefiting the project.
- *Negotiations* – as a project manager you have to negotiate for everything – money, time, resources etc. Your prime objective in negotiations (even if not always labeled as such) is to obtain the stakeholder's support for the project, but a secondary outcome is to understand and adjust their expectations from the project. A successful negotiation always concludes with a win-win solution based on meeting everyone's needs, so don't start the conversation looking for a compromise as nobody will be truly satisfied with it!
- *Informal discussions* – most likely the most powerful tool in your arsenal, given that in casual conversations people tend to open up more than in formal settings. This would allow you not only to get a glimpse behind the scene and adjust the project to meet needs that are not (or cannot be) publicly stated, but also to use your persuasion skills to obtain support and secure approval before getting into a formal path.

- *Indirect influence* – also referred to as political savviness, it represents your ability to use the informal communication paths to influence decision-makers you do not have direct access to, or to set the stage for a future request for project support. Truly understanding your stakeholders, including their sphere of influence, is critical to be able to effectively use the informal channels that exist in any organization. While these activities cannot be usually fully defined in details, based on stakeholders' analysis you should know the key decision-makers that you have limited access to and plan ways of reaching them indirectly.

> *At the beginning of my career in project management I was focused a lot on group activities with the project stakeholders. In retrospect I can say I was organizing a lot of such activities – workshops, brainstorming, presentations etc.*
>
> *It worked for a while, everyone was glad to be involved at the beginning of the project, but not long after reaching execution phase I noticed a certain "fatigue", manifested in a decreased engagement from many stakeholders.*
>
> *Of course, my response at the time was to organize more opportunities for engagement, which translated in more meetings – and even less engagement. To counteract I was doing even more of what I knew (and used to work at the beginning of the project), and – of course – the engagement continued to spiral downwards.*
>
> *It took me couple of years and couple of projects to realize that I was organizing activities for the sake of activities, without having clear objectives in mind for stakeholders' engagement. The activities were geared toward "instinctive" objectives, but these were not defined nor measured.*
>
> *So when the objective was achieved (e.g. they felt that their needs and objectives are clearly understood) they saw no reason to continue to participate in project activities – which I was misinterpreting as diminished engagement. In addition, some people needed a level of attention they were not getting in larger meetings so they stopped attending – and again I was reading wrong that signal.*
>
> *As soon as I started to define clear objectives for stakeholders' engagement, design activities toward reaching specific objectives, and assess progress toward fulfilling them the pieces started to fall in place. The number of group activities decreased significantly as*

I did not overcompensate anymore, and closer monitoring of each (major) stakeholder was indicating if the corresponding objective was reached for them, or specific individual activities are needed for the final touch.

Needless to say, the effort I was putting in it decreased significantly, and the results were incomparably better.

A WHOLISTIC APPROACH

The same as the team members that directly report to you are utilized in different ways throughout the project life-cycle, as a project manager you also have to ensure that stakeholders are engaged in project activities as appropriate for the corresponding project phase.

But it is also important to remember that as project manager you intend to obtain specific results, and for that you must achieve specific objectives – discussed in *Define Activities* section in previous chapter.

If you also decided to use the salience model for stakeholders' classification (Mitchell, Agle, & Wood, 1997), you may end up with a somewhat complex tri-dimensional model, with about 5-7 phases on the life-cycle axis, 7-9 objectives on engagement axis, and 7 classes on the stakeholder axis.

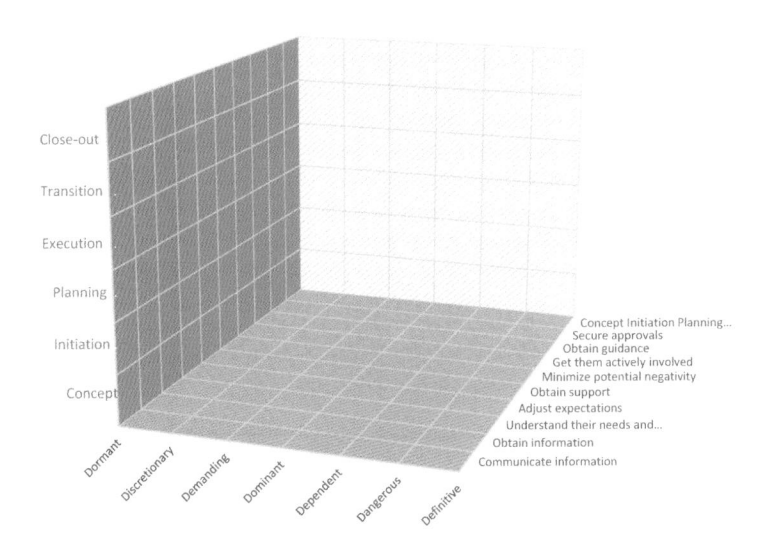

38

The good news: the activities in each cell of the model should have been defined already during the planning exercise, so at this time you should only have to locate the appropriate strategy or strategies to apply.

In practice a 3D model may be a bit cumbersome to use, and it may be simpler to use "slices" through the cube based on one of the axis. The following sample shows the 2D table that corresponds to one of the project phases, e.g. "execution". A similar table would exist for each of the other project phases defined for your project.

Activity \ Stakeholder	Dormant	Discretionary	Demanding	Dominant	Dependent	Dangerous	Definitive
Communicate information	Reports and briefing notes indicating that all is good to keep them dormant	Reports and memos to keep them informed and prevent a movement toward dependent	Reports and memos to keep them informed and prevent a movement toward dependent	Reports and briefing notes providing executive-level status	Reports and memos to keep them informed about meeting their needs	N/A - they have no involvement, sending them information would only imply legitimacy	Presentations, reports, briefings etc. based on individual preferences of receiving information
Obtain information	N/A - not holding anything important	Surveys, polls, questionnaires to understand them as group	N/A - no real interest in the project	Interviews, individual or small group, to provide them the attention they deserve	Surveys, polls, questionnaires for high-level information followed by meetings and interviews only when needed	N/A - they have no involvement, seeking information from them would only imply legitimacy	Workshops, brainstorming, meetings in small group or individual
Understand their needs and expectations	N/A - they typically have none	Surveys, polls, questionnaires to understand them as group	N/A - no real interest in the project	Interviews, individual or small group, to provide them the attention they deserve	Surveys, polls, questionnaires to understand their needs without investing too much time	Indirect influence, to understand that they really want without actually involving them	Workshops, brainstorming, meetings in small group or individual
Adjust expectations	N/A - none to start with	N/A - no power to enforce them anyway	N/A - none to start with	Indirect influence, as they typically listen only to a select number of advisors or peers	N/A - focus on those with power that dependent stakeholders coud try to influence	Indirect influence, as they typically listen only to peers with the same level of power	Negotiations when possible, indirect influence when there is limited access to that stakeholder
Obtain support	Indirect influence and informal discussions to move them toward dominant	N/A - no power to provide support	N/A - no real interest in the project	Negotiations to provide an incentive to get them actively involved	N/A - thyey don't have power to actually support the project	In-person meetings if there is any chance to obtain legitimacy and become a definitive stakeholder	Negotiations when possible, indirect influence when there is limited access to that stakeholder
Minimize potential negativity	N/A - not really having any opinion	Presentations and reports to prevent them feeling unsettled	N/A - no real interest in the project	In-person meetings and negotiations to address their issues	N/A - thyey don't have power to actually hurt the project	In-person meetings and negotiations to address their issues outside the project	Negotiations when possible, indirect influence when there is limited access to that stakeholder
Get them actively involved	N/A - unless you need additional support to counter another powerful stakeholder	N/A - no power to provide support	N/A - no real interest in the project	Negotiations to provide an incentive to get them actively involved	N/A - thyey don't have power to actually support the project	In-person meetings if there is any chance to obtain legitimacy and become a definitive stakeholder	Workshops, brainstorming, simulations for group decisions, presentations and briefing notes for individual decision
Obtain guidance	Interviews, to feel valued and prevent from moving toward dangerous	N/A - no power to enforce their opinion anyway	N/A - no real interest in the project	Interviews, individual or small group, to provide them the attention they deserve	Surveys, polls, questionnaires to understand their high-level objectives	N/A - would only imply legitimacy	Briefings if official direction is needed, informal discussions to "pick their brain"
Secure approvals	N/A - not on the approval list	N/A - not on the approval list	N/A - not on the approval list	In-person briefings to address any individual concerns	N/A - no power to approve	N/A - not part of the approval list	Meetings, presentations, reports, memos, briefing notes, informal discussions, indirect influence etc. as suitable for each stakeholder

39

THE PLAN

Of course, everything previously discussed in this chapter blends together in – of course – a plan. At the first glance it may seem that with all the unknowns and nuances related with dealing with people, as well as the potential sensitivities that you need to account for, it's impossible to put a plan together to describe the approach and activities to obtain the desired stakeholders engagement.

The PMBOK Guide® Fifth Edition introduces the concept of a Stakeholder Management Plan that "identifies the management strategies required to effectively engage stakeholders" (PMI - PMBOK Guide, 2017). The name uses "management" for consistency with the other planning processes and corresponding outputs – and consistency is an important consideration for a standard.

However, you cannot manage what you cannot control, and stakeholders themselves are not within your control as a Project Manager – you can control their engagement by influencing them through the activities described above. As such I use and recommend the term Stakeholders Engagement Plan.

We should remember though that in 2013 it was the first time when the concept that stakeholders are an area that deserves the same level of attention as scope, time, budget etc., so any term that the community could agree with was a significant success. Moreover, at the time there was still significant confusion between Communication and Stakeholders knowledge areas, which is visible in the overlap between their descriptions.

But let's take a look at other plans that you may be more familiar with – let's take the scope management plan and the embedded scope baseline. The baseline represents your best understanding of what the scope looks like (at that specific moment in time), and the plan "describes how the scope will be defined, developed, monitored, controlled and verified" (PMI - PMBOK Guide, 2017).

Applying the same concept, the Stakeholders Register is the baseline for this area as it contains a point-in-time picture of stakeholders and their attributes. As the projects progresses stakeholders are identified or complete their engagement with the project, or change their state as a result of your activities or environmental influences – hence the need to re-baseline.

Following the same logic, the plan would have to describe how stakeholders should be identified, analyzed, engaged, and their engagement monitored to allow adjustments to obtain desired results. While there is no universally accepted structure for this plan (no universally accepted title either), the main topics to be addressed should include:

- *Identify Stakeholders* – define the approach (e.g. top-down or inside-out) and methods (e.g. interviews, questionnaires, and brainstorming) that will be used to ensure that all parties that need to be considered are included on the list of potential stakeholders. Also, you may want to identify who will participate in this exercise, and the criteria to consider the list complete (otherwise it could go on forever).

- *Analyze Stakeholders* – describe the information to be collected about stakeholders, as well as the methods and tools to collect and represent this information and to classify the stakeholders. Remember that some information, or even the knowledge that you'll be collecting some information, can be damaging to the relationship. In these cases you may want to apply the "need to know" concept – even established standards like ISO21500 (ISO\TC258, 2012) and PMBOK Guide (PMI - PMBOK Guide, 2017) clearly state that too much information (more than they need to know) can actually damage efficiency.

- *Engagement Strategy* – define what approach will be applied for group and individual engagement, and what methods will be utilized to support this approach (as discussed in the previous section). The Plan is done for classes of stakeholders, which may include more or less people as defined in the current baseline for the Stakeholder Register – maintained as a separate document. At most specific roles may be listed, but no names should be included in the Plan – who's fulfilling each role at a moment in time is tracked in the Stakeholder Register current baseline.

- *Monitor Engagement* – you cannot manage what you cannot measure, so the most important element to define in this section is how will you know if your approach is successful (the "measuring stick").

Throughout the project you need to reassess the current state of your stakeholders to determine if the strategy and methods applied are obtaining the desired results. The Plan will define how often and how much of the stakeholders' identification and analysis is to be repeated to ensure you have the correct and current picture. Last nu certainly not least, you have to define the triggers that will initiate a re-planning exercise – given the amount of work required you want to do it when needed, but only when needed, and once the project starts it's very easy to miss these signals unless pre-defined in the Plan.

SUMMARY

This chapter presented a few of the tools that I like and use to understand the people I interact with, because each of them provides different perspectives. People are at different career levels, have different personalities, come from different backgrounds etc., so they are both very different and very complex – like diamonds, and each tool will shine the light on only one facet so you'll need a diverse toolset to be able to understand their full intricacies.

And you do need to understand them because – as discussed in previous chapter – the project success depends on their perception about your project. And you'll need individual and group methods able to target the specifics of each stakeholder in order to ensure that the perception they have is the one you want them to have.

It is also essential to set the rules of the game before you start the game – a.k.a. define a Plan. Once the project starts and there are a million things to do it's easy to forget what you should really do, and the Plan is there to guide you about what's important – to not get lost in what's urgent.

You absolutely have to produce the project deliverables, of course. But producing without presenting them, in the hope the stakeholders will take the time to appreciate them, does not guarantee a successful project. You must actively showcase the project's accomplishments, and use multiple methods such as presentations, demos, workshops, brainstorming, reports etc. in order to reach every stakeholder their own way.

To do so efficiently you'll also need as many interpersonal skills as you can master: empathy, communication, negotiation, influencing, persuasion etc. But let's not get ahead of ourselves, we'll talk about all of these in the next chapters of this book as we discuss the main activities the project managers must perform related to stakeholders.

ENGAGE STAKEHOLDERS

Up to this point you identified and analysed the project stakeholders, assesses how you would like them to be to maximize support and minimize resistance, and created a plan of how to get them in the desired state. It is now time to actually do what you planned.

Most literature on this topic calls these processes *Manage Stakeholders*, or *Manage Stakeholders Engagement*. This may be due to the need of consistency with other domains or knowledge areas using the term "manage". However, using this term in relation with stakeholders projects a false illusion of control over something that by definition is outside the Project Manager's ability to command.

Stakeholders are not part of the team you have authority over, and therefore you cannot manage them as you would with the project resources. Moreover, stakeholders' engagement is provided by them at their own free will and control, so you cannot manage stakeholders' engagement either.

The only thing you can really do is to influence the stakeholders to provide on their own accord the desired support for the project. If you properly planned proactive activities (as described in previous chapter), all you have to do is to diligently execute what you planned to create a strong relationship that will withstand occasional friction – because things are not always rosy.

And if you also planned for remedial actions you will know what to do when the storm hits. Of course, as explained in previous chapter, nobody can predict and plan for all the potential issues that could occur during a project – but for those that really matter you should already have a plan for, ready to be enacted without wasting much time in defining options and assess alternatives.

Some will ask "How about the other ones, the ones we did not plan for? Wouldn't they come back to haunt us?" Well, some might – but if you planned for the most serious ones, which would take a significant time to plan for when they happen, the ones not included in the planning stage should be reasonable to assess and respond appropriately when they actually happen.

Of course, all this engagement is done by communicating with the stakeholders. This is a case when the 80/20 rule does not apply, the PM's job is more like 99% communication – to inform, to obtain information, to facilitate decisions, and other engagement elements as suitable.

Humans don't have fangs, or claws, or super-strengths – and still raised as the dominant species on Earth. This is due to our sophisticated communication, unprecedented in the animal world. By working together and communicating to each other we were able to hunt bigger and stronger animals than us, to take care of our youth and expand in all corners of the world. This is still true eve today – in fact, those were projects as well, weren't they?

To conclude, you engage stakeholders by planning, managing or performing specific activities targeted to influence stakeholders toward a desired engagement level, and resolve issues when they occur. This topic is detailed in this chapter, while the next one will describe how to assess if these activities are achieving the desired effect, and how to adjust accordingly.

A NEW COMMUNICATION PARADIGM

The first generally accepted communication model was introduced in 1948 by Claude Shannon (Shannon, 1948) and popularized by Warren Weaver (Weaver & Shannon, 1963). This model was further enhanced by Wilbur Schramm (Schramm, 1954) to describe a three-step process:

- The Sender encodes the meaning into a message using own frameset (experience, knowledge, style, personality etc.) and sends the message to the Receiver
- The Receiver decodes the message through own frameset, processes it and replies to the Sender with what it understood (the reply is encoded with the Receiver's frameset)
- The Sender decodes the reply message through own frameset, compares the feedback with the original intent, and confirms to Receiver that it was correctly understood (or initiates new communication to clarify)

All the above messages are transmitted through same or different communication channels that have various degrees of "noise" impacting the transmission or reception of a message – such as competing messages, transmission method, geography etc.

The following model further expands the concept by adding to each of the 3 basic communication elements an acknowledgement that the message was received – not processed yet, but simply confirming that it reached its destination. This acknowledgement could be implicit (e.g. body language) or explicit (e.g. delivery receipt) based on the type of channel, and confirms that the communication action actually took place.

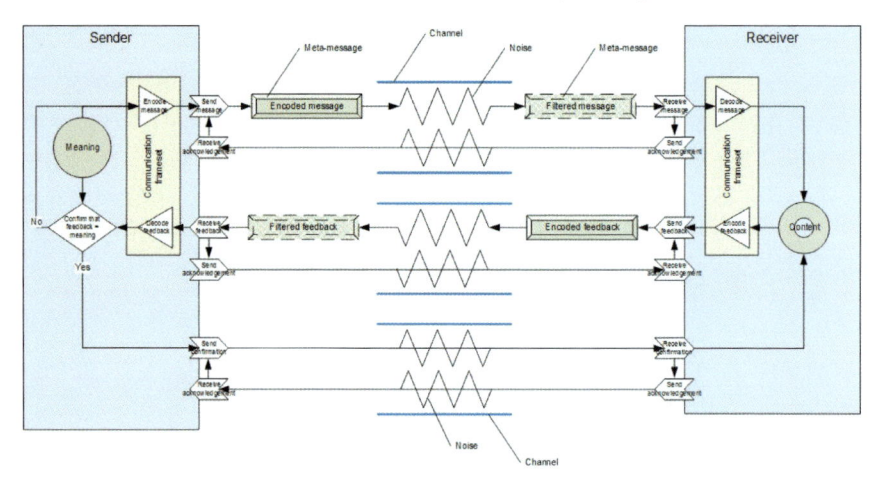

When the participants in a communication process are at the same location, the message originating from the Sender has significant chances to be accurately understood by the receiver. Even if some of the factors that contribute to the encoding frameset are different (e.g. education, cultural background) there are also factors linked to the location that provide some commonality.

During a face-to-face interaction the parties typically pay attention to each other – it is rude for someone to start texting while talking with someone else, but during a conference call nobody sees you! Face-to-face eliminates most of the noise from the medium, and typically enables the message to reach its destination undistorted. Moreover, the message-feedback-acknowledgement loop is practically instantaneous, enabling a rapid conversation flow conducive to large volume of information being exchanged in a short period of time.

However, in today's environment most teams are distributed and engage in virtual communication through audio/video or electronic channels. As if communications wasn't challenging enough already, virtual communication has to face some additional difficulties:

- *Inconsistent encoding/decoding framesets*: except for the people located in the same office (which would employ in-person communication anyway), the team members have few common background elements, which are expected to result in widely different communication framesets, making an encoded message to be very difficult to decode correctly.

- *Intensified noise on the communication channel*: long-distance communication, particularly by email, competes for receiver's attention with multiple other informational streams (given that the "obligation" to pay attention to the person in front of you is now removed). A similar reasoning applies to conference calls as most people multi-task (usually getting through the emails) when calling in from their desk. Even the efficiency of video-conferences, closer to face-to-face meetings, is impacted by awkwardness felt by many while talking to the TV.

- *Incomplete communication (missing non-verbal cues)*: a significant part of the communication is represented by the body language, which allows conveying and perceiving the emotional frame of the spoken message. Even video-conferences cannot properly transmit many non-verbal signals such as facial micro-expressions, body tensing or relaxation, etc., and non-visual communication eliminates the body language completely. This takes away significant elements from the message being transmitted, which need to be replaced with additional verbal communication to explain what could have been communicated by a frown or a smile. Avoiding misunderstandings requires a volume increase of the communication artefact – seven-page emails anyone?

- *Increased lag in the communication cycle*: the separate locations of the team members will most likely push most of the communication to the written channel, such as emails, briefing notes, reports etc. Written communication is asynchronous by definition, with a measurable lag between message and response/feedback, which adds to the time required to resolving the issue at hand. Added to the volume (and associated time) increase described above, this significantly extends the time required to conclude a communication cycle. Even if the delay is only from minutes (face-to-face) to hours (remote), when multiplied with the myriad of issues requiring communication between team members it could add weeks or months to the project schedule.

Interacting with stakeholders, with people in general, requires communication. The traditional communication model includes a vertical and a horizontal dimension: up toward management, down toward the team, and sideways to peers and partners. In reality, it's not only likely but actually expected that project participants will not only communicate with you as the project manager, and sometimes you may not even be part of the communication!

As a project manager you must be very aware that you'll have to manage both the formal communication through organizational channels (meetings, memos, briefings, presentations etc.), but also the informal communication that happens through relationship channels inside (water cooler, coffee line etc.) and outside the office (e.g. lunch).

Communication happens across all dimensions, between all the people involved – up and down, across and all-around! Sometimes with words, sometimes with images, sometimes with gestures, and sometimes even a meaningful silence can be a powerful communication!

If is practically impossible to control or even be part of all the communications that will happen even in the smallest of projects. In fact, trying to do so will only bottleneck communication and slow down or even stop the project.

The key to enabling effective communication is to set the right channels so the people that should talk to each other have an established, open line between them. Moreover, when setting that connection be sure to clearly indicate what subjects or topics can be discussed and what cannot, what type of information is allowable and what requires special approval, and what level of decisions can be made and what needs to be escalated.

This will give people clarity which will generate confidence in actually using the channel. And once all the right communication lines are put in place, there will be almost no need to go outside the process into channels you don't control as people will have all the information they need through what's already available to them (so why spend effort looking for something else?).

As the project manager, you may want to occasionally tap into these communication channels to make sure they did not dry out or are over-flooded with irrelevant communications. If the communication is not flowing efficiently you will have to take on the overhead, so a little bit of proactive work will save you a lot of troubles in the long run.

Last but not least, let's remember that efficient, meaningful communication is not dependent on how much you talk, how many emails you send or how much time you spend in meetings, but on how the communication reaches out to the team members and stakeholders, truly listening to what they have to say, and collaborating on improving the effectiveness and efficiency of working relationships. (Schibi, 2013).

PREVENT AND EXTINGUISH FIRES

When asked to summarize what it means to be a project manager, I usually compare it with an airplane pilot – a pilot has a life of boredom (while the autopilot flies the plane) with occasional moments of terror, while a project manager has a lifetime of terror, with occasional moments of boredom!

In many cases it looks like all that the project manager does is to put out fires while other ones pop up, like a never ending game of whack-a-mole. Everyone seems to have a problem that - of course - is both extremely important and extremely urgent, and needs to be addressed immediately otherwise they threaten to block the project. And the PM just runs from one to another, desperately trying to keep the project moving along!

The work to avoid being in this situation should be done well before the yelling starts, right from the project inception. You must proactively work with stakeholders to understand their needs and expectations, and anticipate these issues before they become problems. The time spent to identify and analyse the stakeholders pays back tenfold in not having to spend time putting out fires later on!

Paying attention to what stakeholders say and don't say is crucial to really understand their motivations and their pain points. Many times they will have nothing to do with the project, but simply find a way and a forum to express accumulated frustrations. As a volcano still boiling, if it has no way to vent it will eventually explode when it finds a crack – with multiplied destructive power!

> *Couple of years ago I was leading a strategic initiative for a public sector organization. When the time came to deploy a software solution supporting the business policy and processes, the support group responsible for deployments reneged the previous work estimates and timelines. The new requests were outrageous, and even if the budget reserve could have covered there was no logical justification for accepting the revised estimates.*
>
> *Trying to reason based on the actual effort / duration of past similar activities always ended in "the past is the past, these are my estimates and I stand by them". Requests for details regarding the estimating technique and details were simply ignored, and there seem to be no way out of the impasse without escalating to executive levels.*
>
> *However, the inflexible attitude made me think at potential subjective issues, and decided to explore this possibility before escalating. Booked a one-on-one meeting with the corresponding manager and, instead of pulling out the scope statement, the schedule etc. I simply asked him "we both know that these estimates are completely unreasonable, so why don't we put them aside and talk about what's really wrong?"*
>
> *Disconcerted by the unexpected approach the manager dropped his guard down and 2-3 probing questions later I figured out the real problem: the department was being reorganized and he was upset that he was not consulted, so he was basically throwing a tantrum and blocking all projects coming his way to get executives' attention.*
>
> *The 30 minutes meeting became a half-day workshop during which he vented off about things that had absolutely nothing to do with my initiative, such as projects coming in late and his group being put under pressure to deliver with less time than needed and looking bad in front of executives because of inherent mistakes. We*

> *discussed other ways to get his ideas for restructuring in front of the executives, and left the meeting without ever bringing up again my problem.*
>
> *When I got back to my office I already had an email confirming some very realistic estimates and timelines that would allow the project to proceed as planned.*

Problems are visible when they create conflict, but when they reach this stage it is already very late – it will take a significant amount of effort and no less negotiating and conflict resolution skills to bring it to satisfactory closure. It is more efficient to uncover issues before they flare up, when there's nothing yet at stake: people will most likely have a polite disagreement over a blueprint, but almost certain a screaming match one half the building was already built!

It is not easy to uncover hot spots before they even send out smoke signals. These are lingering issues, well hidden under a veil of words that have nothing to do with the real bother. In fact, one could say that people invented words not to express their thoughts, but to hide them better!

An effective way to discover many such hot spots is to stimulate conflict as early as possible in the project. The human nature abhors conflict, and most people will instinctively avoid and postpone it as long as possible. However, the issue will not disappear, and postponing will only allow it to grow to a potentially uncontrollable flameout.

Turning every rock early allows to uncover these potential conflicts early, when nothing is at stake yet. At this stage encouraging people to explore potential issues, and sometimes even setting up conflicting scenarios, allows to discuss them calmly and find solutions that truly resolve them rather than just delaying them.

Some good conversations that could uncover potential issues are the project priorities, roles and responsibilities, and project operating framework. Truly exploring these topics by discussing why and not only what should be done will dig down beneath the surface and provide an opportunity to surface discontent that could become a real problem later on.

Once the project starts it is essential to maintain continuous contact with all the key people in the project, to actively collaborate with stakeholders to meet their expectations and address their issues as soon as they occur. Open communication lines allow not only understanding their issues, but also to keep them informed and engaged.

Stakeholders that are truly involved in the project will take steps to resolve their issues immediately. They can adjust project priorities in real time, directly negotiating with the sponsor with an authority that you, as project manager, may never have. New requirements, changes and clarifications are introduced immediately in the scope pool and could be addressed as early as next release / iteration / sprint.

This prevents issues from becoming problems, and keeps them happy – and happy stakeholders translate in successful projects!

EFFECTIVE INVOLVEMENT

Effectively involving stakeholders in the project planning and execution allows the project manager to increase support and minimize resistance from key people, significantly increasing the chances to achieve project success. At the end of the day, if they were a part of it they are partially responsible as well, so how could they declare it anything else but a success?!?

Many project managers are reluctant to open the books and allow the stakeholders access to the inner works of the project planning and execution. Naturally, this creates suspicion that something is going on behind the closed doors, and if it doesn't impact certainly does not help creating and environment of trust.

If you're confident that you're really working toward the project goals why would you hide anything, why not invite the stakeholders into your kitchen to see with their own eyes the hard work done by the team to meet their needs? Truth is, they're probably too busy to do so anyway, but simply knowing that they could do so at any time creates instant trust that the project team is really doing what it's supposed to be doing.

Moreover, active stakeholders' participation in planning and execution results in a better appreciation of challenges, effort required and budgetary consequences. Being an integral part of the decision-making process gains stakeholders' support if changes or corrections are required, and eliminates sign-off anxiety – they already know everything they need to know, so the approvals become a simple formality.

Successful project managers break the barriers between the "team" and "stakeholders" – everyone that has a part to play should be treated as part of "the team". This requires responding to questions and providing input and guidance indiscriminately to stakeholders as well as direct reports. It may require some increased time investment at the beginning of the project, but it will absolutely save your time tenfold later on.

> *Several years back I was hired to manage the IT part of implementing a new legislation. In the very first meeting my business counterpart told me flat out that he's been told to find an outside supplier as the IT organization is completely unreliable.*
>
> *My only recourse was to acknowledge that past performance may not be encouraging, and asked to be given the benefit of the doubt for 3 months to prove that the IT team can be an effective part of this initiative – while subtly pointing out that I already am an "outsider".*
>
> *Unexpectedly, the main challenge was not with the business side but with the IT folks – getting them to abandon the "back room" mentality and actually participate in workshops and brainstorming sessions to define the strategy for the entire initiative, not only for the IT components.*
>
> *It took a lot of encouragement between meetings and engagement during the sessions, by specifically passing questions or topics for discussion to specific people and asking them for their thoughts. In time, people understood that others were genuinely interested in what they have to say and value their opinions, and started to drop their defenses and actively participate.*
>
> *Four years later common sessions were a regular occurrence for all other initiatives, even when they were just concepts considered for potential future programs or legislation.*

Without discounting the technical and technological aspects of the project, a critical success factor of achieving project success is enabling the direct reports and the stakeholders to function as an effective TEAM. While the literature is full of many criteria for efficient teams – all of them important – my past successes were enabled by focusing first and foremost on:

- *Trust and respect* represents the foundation of cohesiveness between the project participants (in any capacity), enabling cooperation and collaboration, efficient communication "at face value" (as opposed to looking for hidden agendas) and expedient conflict resolution.
- *Efficient activities* enabled by clear and shared goals and objectives, well-defined roles and responsibilities, and precise assignments with accountability assumed by the party responsible for delivery.
- *Access to all information* required or relevant to the task at hand or role in the team, provided at the right time and in most efficient format to allow for minimal effort to be obtained, processed and understood.
- *Morale* of each individual and of the team as a whole, actively maintained throughout the entire project by addressing personal goals, expectations and issues that may arise, as well as healthy social interaction within the team and with other stakeholders.

Everyone wants a seat at the table, to be able to have a say in what's impacting them – so make your stakeholders an integral part of "the team" to provide information, guidance and decisions on a timely fashion. This will enable for new requirements, changes and clarifications to shape the project as it is executed to meet evolving stakeholder needs.

If stakeholders can modify project priorities in real time, directly negotiating with the sponsor and project manager, whey will feel committed to the outcomes. This effectively gains stakeholders' support and ensure acceptance as it goes, instead of having to convince them at the end.

YOUR MOST VALUABLE TOOLS

Effectively involving the stakeholders requires you to utilize your entire arsenal of interpersonal skills, based on your understanding of their personalities, way of interpreting information etc. – see *Understanding People* chapter if you need a refresher.

As per PMI, the personal skills mandatory for a competent project manager are (PMI - PMCDF, 2017):

- *Communicating* – the effective exchange of accurate, appropriate and relevant information with stakeholders using suitable methods
- *Leading* – guiding, inspiring and motivating team members and other project stakeholders to manage and overcome issues in order to effectively achieve project objectives
- *Managing* – effective administration of the project through appropriate deployment and use of human, financial, material, intellectual and intangible resources
- *Cognitive Ability* – application of appropriate depth of perception, discernment, and judgement to effectively direct a project in a changing and evolving world
- *Effectiveness* – production of desired results by using appropriate resources, tools and techniques in all project management activities
- *Professionalism* – ethical behaviour governed by responsibility, respect, fairness and honesty in the practice of project management.

One of the elements of "Leading" competence is "uses influencing skills when required", which in my opinion is essential to obtaining an effective stakeholders involvement. At the end of day, you can communicate them all the information they need, when they need it and how they like to receive it, but it you're unable to generate action from their part it's just wasted effort.

There are several good resources out there, but the one that probably influenced me the most is the *How To Win Friends And Influence People* (Carnegie, 1936). With quite a lot of trial and error, I refined over the years my own approach that can be summarized as:

- *Setting the stage* – get ready well before the need to influence even occurs
  - Position yourself in the environment
  - Create your strategic plan based on your objectives

- *Getting started* – once you have identified the need to influence someone to obtain something for your project
    - Prepare your target to be a receptive medium for your future messages
    - Initiate the conversation on the specific topic you need to approach
- Obtain results – using one of the following methods:
    - Logical approach
    - Emotional approach
    - Collaboration approach

SUMMARY

Engaging stakeholders based on the plan described in the previous chapter sounds easier to do than it actually is. Because we're dealing with people, no plan can ever anticipate everything – you can plan based on their typical or usual behaviour, but what if someone has a "bad hair day"?

The key is active and purposeful communication. Even small-talk should have an intent – at least establishing or enhancing the relationship and collecting information about the other person to really know your stakeholders.

In order to get out of the fire-fighting mode that consumes most of your time you have to make a diligent investment into prevention. It may seem that there's never time to become proactive, but you need to find the time even if it means ignoring something else for a while – once you get ahead you'll have plenty of time!

Engaging stakeholders is your time to shine, and make the best out of your interpersonal skills. Truth be told, if you were not a people's person you wouldn't have gotten in project management in the first place!

And don't forget that influencing is a good thing, as long as it's done within ethical boundaries – a.k.a. for the project success and not for personal gain! At the end of the day, our job is to make other people do things that they may not want to do – such as work!

Influencing is the art of making others to <u>want</u> to do what <u>you</u> want them to do!

MONITOR ENGAGEMENT

If you were able to predict the future that accurately so you can plan for every single situation that will be encountered throughout the entire project we wouldn't need to work for another day in your life – with this foretelling ability you could simply play the lottery and win every time!

In real life, we all do our best to think at all possibilities, but it's practically impossible to cover them all. Not only that we never have all the information about everything and everyone involved, but also people are predictable but not quite like machines – to respond in one way and one way only to a specific set of stimuli.

I mentioned couple of times already that the stakeholders' list will change throughout the project. People that seemed to be interested at the beginning may drop off once the scope is defined and it's clear that they're not impacted. Or new people may hear about it and get involved, for good reasons or not.

Continuous, or at least at regular intervals, repeating the stakeholder identification and analysis activities will allow you to update the list of people that you should be focused on, to ensure that you continue to spend effort where it will produce the most productive results.

Our plans, for everything in the project as well as stakeholders' engagement, reflect the best we can do with the information we have at a moment in time. And, as for every other plan, the results produced by the stakeholders' engagement plan will have to be monitored and assessed against desired state or results.

Same as all the other monitoring processes, this requires a continuous or at least regular repeat of stakeholder identification and analysis activities to detect changes in overall project stakeholder list, engagement, relationships, attitudes etc.

And, of course, you will need to adjust your strategies and plans for engaging stakeholders based on current state and upcoming project phases in order to maintain or increase the efficiency and effectiveness of stakeholder engagement activities as the project evolves and its environment changes.

> *In the first years of my career as a Project Manager I discovered the hard way how important the electoral cycle is for long-running public sector projects.*
>
> *Due to longer than expected expenditure approvals (annual reconfirmation of funding and expenditure being another constraint in public sector), the multi-year project was significantly delayed which pushed the implementation date within 6 months of the next elections.*
>
> *I was already working with these stakeholders for 2 years already, and I thought I knew them well. I was feeling comfortable with them, and neglected to pay close attention to their behavior – and being the first time catching an electoral event I did not know what its impact may be either.*
>
> *Long story short, I got surprised by the sudden drop in risk appetite of the top executives. Not only that the scrutiny on project execution and deliverables increased tenfold, but also the project scope came under scrutiny at the 11th hour – with some of the potentially controversial enforcements mechanisms being postponed (even if already done) for a later date (to be determined).*
>
> *If I would have anticipated or at least detected early the change in risk appetite I could have prevented or minimized significantly the tsunami coming our way – but I missed it and it resulted in a lot of last-minute scrambling to reshape everything just before the finish line!*
>
> *However, from this ordeal I learned a very valuable lesson – never get comfortable, anything you know as true today may be false tomorrow!*

DOCUMENT EVERYTHING

Information is power, so making sure you don't miss any significant data element is extremely important to be successful – in general and in engaging stakeholders as well. Personally, I don't like taking minutes and filing everything, and I rely a lot on my own memory and keyword searches to find the information I need.

However, there are several information artefacts that simply must be maintained for any project of significant size – it does consume a significant time when recording the information, but the time savings when you need something more than makes its while!

For me, these artefacts are:

- *Stakeholder register*: changed stakeholders information, new stakeholders identified, registered stakeholders no longer involved in the project
- *Issue log*: updated as new issues are identified and current issues are resolved
- *Stakeholder notifications*: information provided to stakeholders about resolved issues, approved changes, and general project status
- *Project reports*: information formally or informally provided to any or all of the project stakeholders, including project status reports
- *Project records*: correspondence, memos, meeting minutes, and other documents describing the project activities or decisions
- *Feedback from stakeholders*: information received from stakeholders concerning project operations
- *Lessons learned*: includes the root cause analysis of issues faced, reasoning behind the corrective actions etc.

ENGAGEMENT DASHBOARDS

Many other books talk about stakeholders' engagement, but when it comes to monitoring the efficiency of your activities in reaching the desired objectives the advice resumes to re-executing the identify and analyse stakeholders to check their current state.

This is, of course, absolutely necessary, but how do you compare the results with the initial state and – more importantly – with the desired state? This section will focus in providing you with 2 answers to this question, and less on re-running the stakeholders analysis – for a reminder please refer back to chapter *Know Your Stakeholders*, it's exactly the same as you need to do during monitoring.

Given the number of stakeholders in a project, and the multitude of objectives as well as states they could be in, estimating the remaining gap between the current and desired state for each stakeholder could get complicated. Moreover, the ultimate objective is to assess where your attention should be focused for the next period.

For simple projects that do not require a high level of sophistication I use the "Still To-Go" Index (STGI), based on a straight calculation on the SEAM of the number of steps between current and desired states (x_s, where s represents the stakeholder id):

- $C=D \Rightarrow x_s = 0$
- D one step away from C $\Rightarrow x_s = 1$
- D two steps away from C $\Rightarrow x_s = 2$
- and so on.

Stakeholder	Unaware	Resistant	Neutral	Supportive	Leading
1			C		D
2				C/D	
3			C		D
4	C			D	
5		C		D	

C = Current state   D = Desired state

The direction of the arrow does not matter for STGI, only the absolute difference between current and desired state.

> *Resistant ⇢ Neutral ⇢ Supportive ⇢ Leading are in a natural order and it's intuitive how the calculation works. However, Unaware seems to break the pattern – why would it be before Resistant?*
>
> *When moving a stakeholder out from Unaware (a.k.a. they hear about the project), their default position will always be Resistant – a project represents a change which the brain instinctively rejects, and they don't know yet enough about the project to land in any other state.*
>
> *To get an Unaware stakeholder to Neutral would require informing them about the project AND addressing their concerns – so 2 steps. And the logic obviously continues for a desired state of Supportive or Leading.*
>
> *There is a caveat – once moved out from Unaware state a stakeholder can never return to this state – how can someone completely forgot about it? The calculation still stands for desired stated on the left side of current state in SEAM, but Unaware is not a valid desired state.*

And yes, there are instances when we may want to move a stakeholder to the left in SEAM, even in Resistant state! For example, you may seek the support of a more powerful stakeholder, which already is in conflict with another one of your stakeholders – so influencing one to become Resistant is a sure way for the other to become Supportive or even Leading!

The STGI can be done for each stakeholder or even by groups or classes, depending on the stakeholders' analysis and planning of engagement activities. Also, it uses a weighting system (w_s, where *s* represents the stakeholder id) to show the relative importance of stakeholders – it could be a simple ranking scale or a points system based on your preference.

The STGI for each stakeholder is a simple weighted SEAM score:

$STGI_s = x_s * w_s$, where *s* represents the stakeholder id.

The outcome can be presented in a table or a graph – I personally prefer the visual representation of how much it is "still to go" to reach the 0-line where C=D, allowing to focus the attention to the problem areas.

Stakeholder / Class	Weight	SEAM Score	STGI
Dormant	1	2	-2
Discretionary	2	1	-2
Demanding	2	3	-6
Dominant	2	2	-4
Dependent	1	1	-1
Dangerous	3	1	-3
Definitive	3	0	0

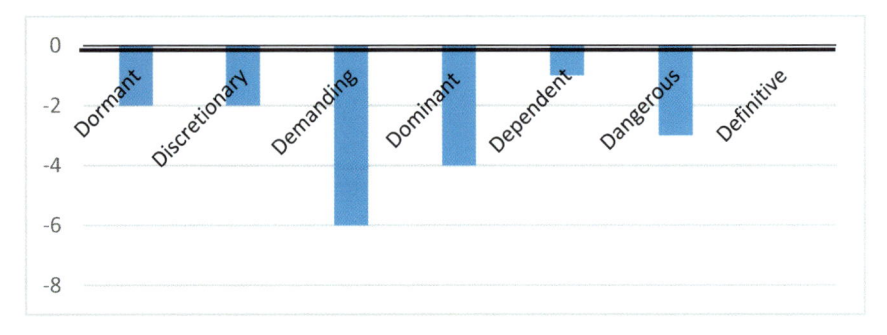

For more complex projects, the STGI simple calculation does not provide enough granularity to provide fine-tuned approaches to engaging stakeholders. In this case I use a more complex matrix that calculates the Stakeholders' Heat Map, the Stakeholder Activities Performance Index (SAPI) and the Stakeholder Engagement Performance Index (SEPI).

The Heat Map calculates a double-weighted score and visually represents the efficiency in reaching the engagement objectives for each stakeholder or class of stakeholders.

It is represented as a matrix that uses on the horizontal dimension the stakeholders' names, groups or classes. They can be mixed – for example, most stakeholders are represented through their group/class as identified during analysis, but for some stakeholders we may want to have special monitoring.

> *In a mixed case the stakeholders' analysis and engagement planning should be revised to ensure that the "individual" stakeholders are NOT included in a group/category as well – otherwise they could receive conflicting messages due to individual and group activities.*

Similar with STGI method, a weighting system (w_s, *where s represents the stakeholder id*) of your choosing should be used to distinguish the relative importance of corresponding stakeholders or classes.

On the horizontal dimension the matrix lists the engagement objectives defined in planning – see *Define Activities* section for a reminder. These also have a weighting system (w_o, *where o represents the objective id*) applied, to represent their relative importance for the specific project.

During the assessment each cell receives a points-score (p_{so}, *where s represents the stakeholder id and o represents the objective id*) between -2 (very bad) and +2 (very good). This score is assigned based on predefined criteria for each project. For example:

Communicate information	-2 = no acknowledgement -1 = occasional acknowledgement 0 = acknowledged if requested 1 = regularly acknowledged 2 = almost always acknowledged
Obtain information	-2 = almost never -1 = hard to get 0 = requires follow-up 1 = complete and in time 2 = volunteer information
Understand their needs and expectations	-2 = no clue, avoid expressing them -1 = obtained through escalation 0 = requires multiple probing questions 1 = provided when asked 2 = volunteer disclosure
Adjust expectations	-2 = no change whatever you try -1 = obtained through escalation 0 = requires multiple conversations 1 = agreed if explained 2 = self-initiated based on information
Obtain support	-2 = no support, no way -1 = obtained through escalation 0 = requires negotiations 1 = provided when asked 2 = voluntary offered
Minimize potential negativity	-2 = outspoken against the project -1 = passive resistance 0 = requires negotiations 1 = stopped when explained 2 = self-changed based on information
Obtain active participation	-2 = no participation whatsoever -1 = only if directed from above 0 = time permitting 1 = when asked personally 2 = almost always
Obtain guidance	-2 = no advice whatsoever -1 = rarely and incomplete /unclear 0 = requires follow-ups 1 = provided when asked 2 = voluntary offered
Secure approvals	-2 = no approval, no way -1 = obtained through escalation 0 = requires negotiations 1 = provided when asked 2 = voluntary offered

The scores can be assigned by you based on own observation, or you can use a method such as Delphi technique to combine the inputs from your project management team. This allows to introduce a layer of objectivity in a fundamentally subjective exercise.

A typical input matrix for the Heat Map would look like:

Activity	Stakeholder	Dormant 1	Discretionary 1	Demanding 2	Dominant 2	Dependent 1	Dangerous 3	Definitive 3
Communicate information -2 = no acknowledgement -1 = occasional acknowledgement 0 = acknowledged if requested 1 = regularly acknowledged 2 = almost always acknowledged	1	0	-1	2	2	-2	-1	0
Obtain information -2 = almost never -1 = hard to get 0 = requires follow-up 1 = complete and in time 2 = volunteer information	1	2	0	-1	-2	1	0	1
Understand their needs and expectations -2 = no clue, avoid expressing them -1 = obtained through escalation 0 = requires multiple probing questions 1 = provided when asked 2 = volunteer disclosure	2	-1	-2	0	-1	1	1	2
Adjust expectations -2 = no change whatever you try -1 = obtained through escalation 0 = requires multiple conversations 1 = agreed if explained 2 = self-initiated based on information	2	1	0	1	-2	2	-1	0
Obtain support -2 = no support, no way -1 = obtained through escalation 0 = requires negotiations 1 = provided when asked 2 = voluntary offered	2	2	-2	2	0	0	-1	-2
Minimize potential negativity -2 = outspoken against the project -1 = passive resistance 0 = requires negotiations 1 = stopped when explained 2 = self-changed based on information	3	-2	1	0	1	2	0	1
Obtain active participation -2 = no participation whatsoever -1 = only if directed from above 0 = time permitting 1 = when asked personally 2 = almost always	3	-1	1	1	2	-1	-2	0
Obtain guidance -2 = no advice whatsoever -1 = rarely and incomplete /unclear 0 = requires follow-ups 1 = provided when asked 2 = voluntary offered	2	-2	2	-1	0	1	0	1
Secure approvals -2 = no approval, no way -1 = obtained through escalation 0 = requires negotiations 1 = provided when asked 2 = voluntary offered	3	2	1	-1	-2	0	1	2

To account for the relative importance of stakeholder and engagement objectives, this score is multiplied with the respective stakeholder and objective weight to obtain the corresponding cell's Heat Map Index (HMI):

$HMI_{so} = p_{so} * w_s * w_o$, where s represents the stakeholder id and o represents the objective id

The Heat Map is colored based on ranges of positive and negative values. The following example uses 1/2/3 weighting for both stakeholders and objectives, and the resulting Heat Map indicates the areas that need most attention (colored in a darker shade of red).

Stakeholder\Activity	Dormant 1	Discretionary 1	Demanding 2	Dominant 2	Dependent 1	Dangerous 3	Definitive 3	SAPI
Communicate information	1							2
Obtain information	1							0
Understand their needs and expectations	2							10
Adjust expectations	2							-4
Obtain support	2							-10
Minimize potential negativity	3							18
Obtain active participation	3							-3
Obtain guidance	2							4
Secure approvals	3							18
SEPI	-1	4	10	-6	10	-18	36	

Stakeholder Activities Performance Index (SAPI) and the Stakeholder Engagement Performance Index (SEPI) are calculated as horizontal and vertical sums of HMI_{SO}, as seen in the example above.

SAPI illustrates the efficiency of activities executed for each engagement objective across all the project stakeholders.

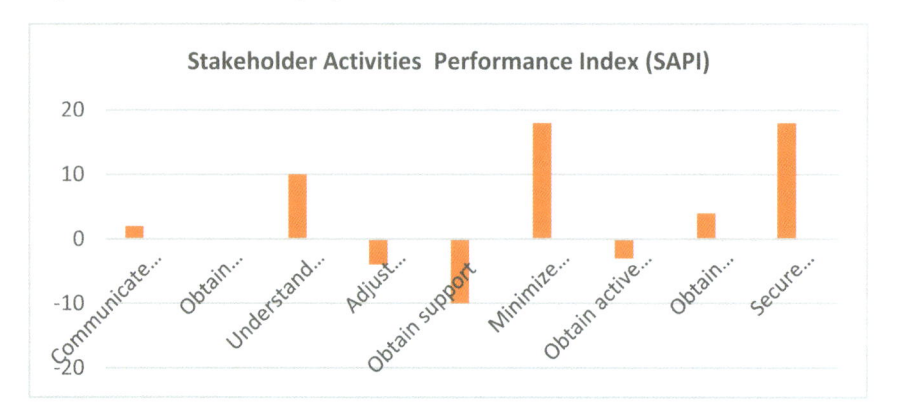

SEPI shows which stakeholders are being efficiently impacted by engagement activities and which ones may require more attention.

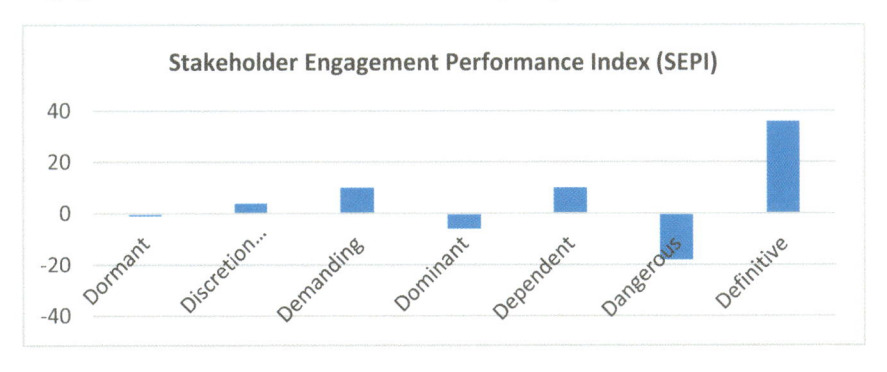

Stakeholder Engagement Performance Index (SEPI)

[Bar chart showing values for: Dormant, Discretion..., Demanding, Dominant, Dependent, Dangerous, Definitive, ranging from approximately -20 to 35]

ADJUST YOUR STRATEGIES

At this point you have assessed the current state of stakeholders' engagement and compared with where you need them to be – and maybe even identified the areas you should focus on by using one of the dashboards described above.

Now it's time to ask yourself what activities performed to date produced the intended result, and which ones did not? And then you need to as Why? – both for the ones that worked out and for the ones that didn't, so you can understand what to repeat and also what to change.

As a quick reminder, some of the activities that you can perform, as discussed in section *Define Activities*, are

Individual Activities:	Group Activities:
Interviews, one-on-one	Meetings, workshops
Briefings, information notes	Group decision techniques
Negotiations	(brainstorming, Delphi etc.)
Informal discussions	Surveys, questionnaires, polls
Direct or indirect influence	Presentations
	Reports, memos, briefings
	Simulations, demonstrations

In some cases, you may need to adjust the activity performed to produce better results. In other cases you may need to change to a complete new activity, and even from a group to an individual activity or vive-versa (there are people that are not comfortable being approached individually, they feel safer in a group setting)!

Sounds extremely complex – and it is, but you should remember that you are not alone! You don't need to bear the weight of the world solely on your shoulders, you can ask for help and get other people involved in defining the best approach to engage other stakeholders.

Some of the people I go to and ask for help in reshaping the activities to obtain a desired result, sometimes providing details and sometimes describing "a hypothetical scenario", are:

- Senior management that have a wider perspective and reach throughout the organization
- Already engaged key stakeholders – they have all interest for the project to succeed!
- Team members that may have worked with the "target" stakeholders in the past
- Other units or individuals within the organization
- Project managers who have worked on projects in the same area (directly or through lessons learned)
- Subject matter experts in the business or project area
- Industry groups and consultants that may have faced similar scenarios

In fact, asking for help in dealing with an impasse is a useful influencing technique – the least you get is information, but you may also prompt the person you ask for help to get involved and deal with the issue for you!

SUMMARY

Like a high-performance engine, stakeholder engagement activities must be monitored and fine-tuned throughout the entire project life-cycle. Stakeholders are people, and people change – sometimes for good reasons but quite often without any visible justification!

While you may not always understand the real reason of the change, you should always be on the lookout for the external signs of change and adjust the engagement activities accordingly. Of course, it's always better if you can find and address the root-cause, particularly if it's related to your project.

For this, continuous or at least regular repeat of the stakeholder identification and analysis is key, as is the progress toward meeting the engagement objectives for each stakeholder or class of stakeholders. We talked about some useful tools to dashboard the current state of engagement – STGI for simpler projects, and Heat Map, SAPI and SEPI for more complex situations.

If defining the engagement activities during planning was hard, adjusting them for performance is even harder – now you have to assess how effective they were or not, and find out why they were or not effective. And once you understand you need to find the required adjustment, or another activity that will allow reaching your objectives.

It is a daunting task, but if you diligently capture the relevant information about stakeholders and enroll the help of more people it becomes like a great symphony! The conductor leads the entire thing, but also has help in each area to influence the others (e.g. the first violin, or the drums that keep the cadence for everyone).

From my personal experience I can assure you that, despite the fact that at the beginning is hard, it becomes very quickly a way of life and you'll perform the monitoring and adjustment without even realizing it. But what you'll see are the results in the attitudes of the people involved in the project!

TOP 5 TIPS FOR EFFECTIVE ENGAGEMENT

CHANGE ~~MANAGEMENT~~ ENABLEMENT

Many project managers (and not only) treat change management as being "change resistance", fighting to prevent change from happening in the project in order to deliver as per approved baselines. This is a fundamental contradiction in concepts, as a project is all about introducing change, so why would the change not be changed again?

Moreover, if we had the ability to predict exactly what will happen six months, a year or two in the future we would be amazing foretellers – we could simply play the lottery and never have to work another day!

There is nothing more powerful than change and "resistance is futile", so we need to remain flexible throughout the entire project to embrace change. In fact, these adjustments allow the project to keep up with changing realities and supply what the users need at the time of delivery, not what was put on paper months or years ago.

Change means evolution so it's not necessarily bad – especially if properly managed. In fact:

Changes are good, <u>unmanaged</u> changes are bad!

Energies spent on preventing changes (unsuccessfully) would be better used to incorporate change with minimal disruptions. Your role is to put in place a foundation of enabling managed changes rather that preventing them, allowing change to be constructive rather than destructive to the project!

Remember that stakeholders initiating change don't particularly care if the change is managed or not – they simply want the easier way for them to achieve their objective. Creating more formal processes and elaborate procedures will drive the change underground – not visible and therefore not controlled – as people don't really enjoy all the extra effort they have to put in to push the change through.

If instead you reduce the "red tape" required for changes to be introduced in the project by simplifying procedural steps, forms and approvals you will be able to attract the requested changes under control. People will always take the path of least resistance – they will follow the process as long as the "official way" requires less effort than inventing a way to go around the process.

Lastly, many project managers feel overprotective toward the project scope, and anyone threatening it is perceived as a personal attack. We need to always remember that the responsibility for the project scope resides with the client – the project only borrows it for a while but at the end it transfers it back to the organization.

So our role as project managers is to provide a clear impact assessment of desired change to enable informed decisions, and once the decision is made introduce the change (if so decided) as soon as practical for minimal impact. And then we have another baseline to protect – until the next change, that is!

FIRST AGREE ON PROCESSES

During the initiation and planning phases most conflicts occur from negotiations about the project objectives and priorities – and those are healthy conflicts that shape the deliverables to be achieved. Once the execution phase starts, most conflicts occur due to various and inconsistent interpretations of the "game rules" – and these are noise at best and disruptions in the worst case scenario.

It is quite often that processes to be followed and deliverables to be achieved get intermingled and confuse participants, preventing consensus achievement – or worse. Issues will occur, and ad-hoc processes promoted a party trying to resolve their issue may antagonize other parties that feel that they are not treated as equals.

This will detract focus from achieving deliverables toward establishing processes. And when the outcome is in sight, any discussion about the process will be undermined by suspicions of skewing the process to obtain a desired result – much like two teams arguing after the puck got in the net if the puck has to touch, completely pass or just the middle to pass the line to be a valid goal! There's already plenty of arguments with the rules already in place, can you imagine defining the rules in the middle of the play?

Set the rules before you start the game!

To avoid (most of) these disruptive conflicts critical process need to be commonly agreed at the very beginning of the project, with the participation of all stakeholders. It is easier to agree on processes at the beginning of the project, when nothing is at stake – nothing was built yet, no (significant) money were spent, so people will perceive this more or less as a theoretical exercise.

It is your interest to guide the stakeholders toward consensus on how to communicate, how to work together, how to make decisions and so on – otherwise it's you that will be in the middle of all conflicts generated by lack of clarity. And it's important to achieve consensus, not use majority voting – discontent people will always argue later that "I never agreed to this" and the conflict is back on! But remember, consensus is defined as "everybody can live with it" and not "everybody agrees with it", otherwise it can never be achieved!

The agreed "rules of the game" must be documented in a procedural framework and formally approved by all stakeholders – memory is a funny thing, three people coming out from a meeting will remember four versions of what was agreed on (pun intended). Once agreed, processes should be consistently applied and never be revisited when a deliverable is at stake.

In fact, the procedural framework should not be touched until the project ends. However, if a challenge is raised during the project to the level that it may jeopardize consensus (and therefore delivery) it is essential to apply the "old" framework for any item currently under discussion, and only allow procedural discussions to happen only when there's nothing at stake.

You want it or not, you like it or not, you're the referee and you cannot do your job without a solid set of rules to enforce during the game!

SINGLE VERSION OF THE TRUTH

In 1597, Sir Francis Bacon wrote in his *Meditationes Sacrae* that "ipsa scientia potestas est" – in translation "knowledge itself is powerful" (Bacon, 1884). The knowledge economy of the 21st century has clearly proved him right – and that is just as true in projects as it is for the entire society.

Knowledge (including information) management is critical to ensure a common understanding about the project status and planned activities. Without information that is consistent, complete and available each team member or stakeholder will fill in the blanks with assumptions – and I hope you remember from the beginning that people hear what they want to hear, and see what they want to see!

Half-truths (from real information) filled in with assumptions consistent with the personal frameset of values will be perceived as a whole truth. Moreover, this will support or cause people to move in an "assumed" direction, with total confidence that this is the right direction. And if any others move in a different direction, tough luck – they are surely wrong!

Information is power – use it!

As a project manager, you must control the information flowing through the project – but if you recall the communication paradigm introduced earlier in this book much of the information flows *around* you between the various people involved with the project. So how can you control something that you're not even part of?

The first step should be done at the beginning of the project, while defining the communication channels to be used between various participants. It is important to specify not only the participants in the corresponding information exchange, but also what topics are to be discussed through this channel and, maybe even more importantly, what is not to be discussed but escalated – and to whom it should be escalated to.

This will capture most communication into the defined channels – people will not spend the effort of creating new channels (locate the right person or persons, set up meetings etc.) if they already have something available to them to obtain and provide information. It will not capture it all though, there will always be some "uncontrolled" communication that could be problematic – either too much information, out of context or simply erroneous.

To counteract the questionable information you must ensure that all participants know how to obtain the official, verified information. The simplest method is to create a central, shared repository to maintain a single version of truth for common reference and continuously remind people to validate any information they receive against the content of the shared repository.

ENABLE VOLUNTARY COMPLIANCE

Adherence to formal processes is extremely difficult to impose on stakeholders, especially when the processes don't seem natural, clear and easy to follow. To make sure that rules are followed you need to enable voluntary compliance rather than enforcement – you certainly catch more flies with honey than vinegar!

Try to push someone from their place – they will instinctively resist, even if moving may be a good thing for them. Based on this resistance, some will conclude that people hate change as a concept, before they even consider if it's positive or negative.

Complex environments and initiatives increase the need for formal processes to ensure cohesiveness. However, trying to change existing processes or introduce new ones will be met with resistance – which could generate conflicts that will significantly slow down or even block the project.

On the other hand, we know that people change jobs, change houses and cars, marry, have children and so on – all major changes, and people not only don't resist but actually embrace them! The difference is that they initiated the change, it comes from within rather than being enforced onto them from outside!

**People don't hate change,
they hate being changed!**

Once the fundamental paradigm is changed the approach must be adjusted as well. Start to engage stakeholders in defining the processes so they are part of them, rather than subject to them. Even if you have to apply "organizational" processes, they are never as rigid as they may seem at the first glance – and at minimum you can engage the stakeholders to discuss how do "we" deal with them.

This establishes not only a common understanding of processes and ways to cope with them, but also a sense of togetherness by rallying against a "common foe". Through these discussions they will find ways of doing things that change their old ways – but that's OK, because now these are perceived as <u>their</u> changes, not something imposed from outside (even if in fact they actually are due to an outside pressure).

People that worked through the processes and activities required, and came to a consensus solution (a.k.a. they agreed with it) are now invested – it is their solution, they believe in what they defined so they will do their best to adhere to them even without supervision or coercion. Not doing so would negate their own solution, and not many people would easily accept that they were wrong…

Of course, as the Project Manager you need to influence the process (without taking over) to make sure that the right topics are being addressed and resolved, and as much as possible close to your own way of doing things. It is a delicate balance to maintain, if you push too hard you take over and it's not "theirs" anymore, if not enough you may not get to any results and it becomes just a waste of time.

At minimum, the following areas should be discussed and processes / procedures agreed upon:

- How to work together – roles, responsibilities, relationships
- How to exchange information – tools, medium, frequency
- How to identify and resolve issues – collaboration and escalation
- How to track progress – delivery status, forecasts, impacts
- How to resolve conflicts – negotiation and arbitration rules

AVOID ROADBLOCKS

Projects bring about change in the organization, breaking the molds to introduce something new, which was not there before. At the same time, organizations are fundamentally focused on stability – they need consistency to be able to run effective operations.

It stands to reason that organizations will create barriers and obstructions for projects in order to minimize disruptions, sometimes even without realizing that they do so. They may call them checkpoints, kill points or stage gates, and may even claim that the super-formal processes with tens of checkboxes and documents are for the good of the projects.

Let me be very clear – I'm not an advocate of Wild West project management, some checks and balances are required both for project's and for organization's sake. But you need to be aware of all roadblocks that your project will inherently be faced with, sometimes visible and sometimes not.

As project teams are usually formed by people driven to bring about change, all these roadblock will create tension in the team. Adding this to the incertitude inherent to any project, it creates a highly-charged environment that you, as the project manager, need to deal with.

As there will be enough tension in the project anyway, there is no need to add even more procedural roadblocks to the contributing factors. Quite the opposite, your role is to find a way to ease off the burden where you can, and to help people through the process where you cannot change it.

> *Getting ready to manage my very first project I created all the tools and templates that I could possibly need. I was particularly proud of the impact assessment within the change management process – it was quite comprehensive and I hoped I captured all the possible review angles to determine even the slightest chance of impact.*
>
> *Not long after the project started the first change request comes in – a small one, but it took the equivalent of 8 person/days to perform the assessment. The team got it out in 3 calendar days, which wasn't bad at all.*
>
> *But then the change requests started to pour in due to a new regulation that required significant changes in the business*

> *process. There was no more time to do any work, the entire team was dedicated to assessing changes – and in many cases the originator would not like the assessment and change the request, and we would have to run the assessment again!*
>
> *Not only that the team's frustration was growing exponentially each day, but also – because so many requests were blocked in the pipeline by the over-complicated assessment – it created significant frustration in the stakeholders' community and conflict with the project team.*
>
> *I was too young and proud to accept my mistake, so eventually the project sponsor had to step in and direct me to streamline the process. But ever since I always start with the bare minimum, and add more if really needed, rather that repeat that mistake again.*

To avoid or minimize frustrations you need to get the stakeholders to actively participate in defining the most efficient processes that can be put in place within the project given organizational roadblocks. Being part of the definition creates accountability to follow them, and eliminates the incertitude from "unknown" rules.

This requires not only full transparency, by communicating how, what, when, who and why, and also manage their expectations – now they know what they're dealing with. And if you also create effective methods to solicit, receive, process and act on feedback, they will be confident in their ability to influence the processes – minimizing their frustration and increasing their support toward the project.

CONCLUSIONS

Stakeholder Engagement is (arguably) the most underestimated area of project management – and yet so decisive for achieving project success. Effectively engaging stakeholders can make or break a project – more than any methodology, tools or techniques.

Good stakeholder engagement results in:

- Efficient communications, focused on project activities, with less time wasted in explanations.
- Introduced changes have positive rather than negative impact on the project.
- Support and ownership are high and lead to easier acceptance and increased usage of deliverables.

As any other area of project management, stakeholders' engagement requires a systemic and sustained approach that includes:

- Know your stakeholders.
- Plan stakeholder engagement.
- Engage stakeholders.
- Monitor engagement.

Working with people is both difficult and extremely rewarding – as long as it is performed within ethical boundaries, for the benefit of the project and not for personal gain. You will need to know and use a wide variety of tools and methods to really understand what makes them tick, and a wide range of interpersonal skills to interact with them.

As a reward for making it this far, please visit the Knowledge Library at http://openablers.net/knowledge.php to the book's page to download the templates featured in this book for FREE – not even registration required, no need to sign for any mailing list, simply download for free!

And there is no better way to conclude than sharing my secret for a successful career – I call it the Roadmap to Project Success:

Stakeholders
- Project success is measured in stakeholders satisfaction.

Support
- Stakeholders need to be "part of the team" to truly support the project.

Exercises
- Stakeholders happiness is directly proportional with their ability to exercise change.

Change
- Change is the only constant throughout the entire project - build processes based on enabling change, not against it.

Enabling
- Enabling change allows to deliver what they really need, not what they thought they want when the project started.

Success
- Meeting the stakeholder needs results in a **successful project**!

ABOUT THE AUTHOR

George Jucan is well known in the project management community as a successful consultant, public speaker, trainer and author, with over 25 years of maximizing value delivery in a broad range of endeavours within many business areas, in large and complex public and private sector environments.

He is an internationally recognized project management expert, currently being the Chair of the Canadian Mirror Committee at International Organization of Standardization (ISO) for the Project, Programme and Portfolio Management set of standards, and International Convener of ISO\TC258\WG3. George also had multiple leadership positions in PMI Standard Committees, including PMBOK® Guide 6th, 5th and 4th Editions, PMCDF 2nd Edition and Government Extension to the PMBOK® Guide 3rd Edition.

An expert in motivating people and building relationships across organizational boundaries with all stakeholders – executives, customers, team and delivery partners, George successfully defined strategic roadmaps, optimized processes and reorganized departments for efficiency. He also managed award-winning projects in challenging stakeholder environment, delivering complex solutions that met not only requirements but the actual business needs and objectives that generated the initiative in the first place.

George has a passion for sharing his knowledge and experience with the community – he previously contributed to two books and published numerous articles. A highly entertaining and engaging speaker, his sessions are extremely interactive and create a personal connection with 500 people audiences as well as 50. He brings in his extensive personal experience to enhance the message and reach the participants' minds and hearts alike.

BIBLIOGRAPHY

Bacon, F. (1884). *The Works of Francis Bacon, Volume 1.* New York:: R. Worthington.

Carnegie, D. (1936). *How To Win Friends And Influence People.*

Cleland, D. I. (Ed.). (2004). *A Field Guide to Project Management* (2nd ed.). New Jersey: John Wiley & Sons, Inc.

Cook Briggs, K., & Briggs Myers, I. (1962). *The Myers-Briggs Type Indicator: Manual.* Consulting Psychologists Press.

ISO\TC258. (2012). ISO 21500:2012 - Guidance on project management. ISO.

Jung, C. G. (1921). *Psychological Types.* Zurich: Rascher Verlag.

Kolb, D. A. (1984). *The experiential learning: Experience as the source of learning and development.* FT Press.

Luft, J., & Ingham, H. (1955). The Johari window, a graphic model of interpersonal awareness. *Proceedings of the western training laboratory in group development.* Los Angeles: University of California, Los Angeles.

Maslow, A. (1943). A Theory of Human Motivation. *Psychological Review.*

Maslow, A. (1954). *Motivation and Personality.* New York: Harper & Brothers.

Mitchell, R., Agle, B., & Wood, D. (1997). Toward a Theory of Stakeholder Identification and Salience: Defining the Principle of Who and What Really Counts. *The Academy of Management Review*, 507-525.

PMI - PMBOK Guide. (2017). *A Guide to the Project Management Body of Knowledge (PMBOK® Guide)—Sixth Edition, 6th.* Project Management Institute.

PMI - PMCDF. (2017). *Project Manager Competency Development Framework (PMCDF) - Third Edition* (3rd ed.). Project Management Institute.

Roeder, T. (2013). *Managing Project Stakeholders: Building a Foundation to Achieve Project Goals.* Wiley.

Schibi, O. (2013). *Managing Stakeholder Expectations for Project Success: A Knowledge Integration Framework and Value Focused Approach.* J Ross Publishing.

Schramm, W. L. (1954). How communication works. In W. L. Schramm, *The process and effects of mass communication.* University of Illinois Press.

Scott, L. (2013). *Gower Handbook of People in Project Management.* Gower.

Shannon, C. E. (1948). A Mathematical Theory of Communication. *Bell System Technical Journal, 7.*

Sternberg, R. J. (1985). *Beyond IQ: A Triarchic Theory of Intelligence.* Cambridge: Cambridge University Press.

Weaver, P., & Bourne, L. (2002). Concepts for a 'Stakeholder Circle' Management Tool. *PMI Melbourne Chapter Conference.* Melbourne.

Weaver, W., & Shannon, C. E. (1963). *The Mathematical Theory of Communication.* University of Illinois Press.

Printed in Great Britain
by Amazon